S0-CFM-781

Wicked Washington

Mysteries, Murder & Mayhem in America's Capital

Troy Taylor

Published by The History Press
Charleston, SC 29403
www.historypress.net

Cover design by Marshall Hudson.

First published 2007

Manufactured in the United States

ISBN 978.1.59629.302.1

Library of Congress Cataloging-in-Publication Data

Taylor, Troy.
Wicked Washington : mysteries, murder & mayhem in America's capital / Troy Taylor.
p. cm.
Includes bibliographical references.
ISBN 978-1-59629-302-1 (alk. paper)
1. Washington (D.C.)--History--Anecdotes. 2. Washington (D.C.)--Social conditions--Anecdotes. 3. Washington (D.C.)--Biography--Anecdotes. 4. Politicians--Washington (D.C.)--Biography--Anecdotes. 5. Scandals--Washington (D.C.)--History--Anecdotes. 6. Corruption--Washington (D.C.)--History--Anecdotes. 7. Murder--Washington (D.C.)--History--Anecdotes. 8. Crime--Washington (D.C.)--History--Anecdotes. 9. Criminals--Washington (D.C.)--Biography--Anecdotes. I. Title.
F194.6.T395 2007
975.3--dc22
2007035340

Contents

Introduction

There are some who would frown at the idea of me referring to our beloved nation's capital as "wicked." We don't see wickedness as we gaze on the magnificent dome of the Capitol building or along the stretch of the Washington Mall. This is not a city like Chicago, with her long history of blood and corruption, or New Orleans, with her centuries of ghosts, pirates and voodoo. This is Washington, America's seat of power, where laws are created and where great men walk the streets or stare down at us from the marble seats of towering monuments. This should be a place where the sun that shines off the polished stone is only half as bright as the sterling reputation of this great city.

But, of course, this is not the case.

Washington, like other American cities that are steeped in legend and lore and stained with blood, has a past. It is a past that is unlike that of any other city in our nation, from the methods that were used to build her to the scandals, deaths and corruption that have so captured our imagination. As the reader will soon discover, the description of "wicked" for Washington is one that is especially fitting!

The city of Washington is a place of strangeness and contradictions. It is the capital of the United States, but it exists in a place that is not actually a state. It is the center of our nation's laws, and yet for many years, the residents of the city were unable to vote in national elections. For decades the city was so unhealthy that thousands of deaths (including that of Abraham Lincoln's son) were blamed on the unsanitary conditions of the streets and waterways. Despite its reputation as a "shining beacon of democracy," most realized the city had a dark side too. One writer stated that: "Washington is the nation's gothic capital, the shining city on a haunted hill."[1]

The first settlers in Washington were Native Americans who came to the area more than four thousand years ago. Their descendants were later pushed out of the region by the Europeans, who expanded the Virginia colony from the south and the province of Maryland from the east. While the central portion of the future city was largely uninhabitable wetlands, two port towns appeared nearby, on opposite sides of the Potomac River. Georgetown was first settled in 1706, and the city of Alexandria came along years later in 1749. Two smaller settlements also started nearby. They were Carrollsburg and Hamburgh, a small collection of houses that was located near the present-day site of the state department headquarters in Foggy Bottom.

After the end of the Revolutionary War in 1783, the new American government met in New York and Philadelphia. Rivalry between the states to be home to a new, permanent capital led the 1787 Constitutional Convention to empower Congress to create a new federal district that would not be part of any state. The location for the new capital was chosen by the time-honored method of political maneuvering. It happened over a dinner between Thomas Jefferson and Alexander Hamilton. Jefferson agreed to support Hamilton's banking and federal bond plans, which involved the government assuming state's debts in exchange for Hamilton's support of the nation's capital being in a southern locale.

On December 23, 1788, the Maryland General Assembly allowed the state to cede land for the federal district. The Virginia General Assembly waited almost a full year before they also relinquished land. The signing of the Residence Act of 1790 mandated a site for the seat of government that did not exceed "ten miles square" (one hundred square miles) and that was located on the "River Potomac, at some place between the mouths of the Eastern Branch and the Connogocheque." This act authorized the president of the United States to select the actual location.

Once again, politics would play a role in the manipulation of the site. President George Washington wanted to include the town of Alexandria, Virginia, within the square federal district that had been authorized by the act. To accomplish this, the boundaries of the district would have to be moved to encompass an area on the Potomac River that was downstream from the mouth of the Eastern Branch (now the Anacostia River), and subsequently, they would not fall between the "mouths of

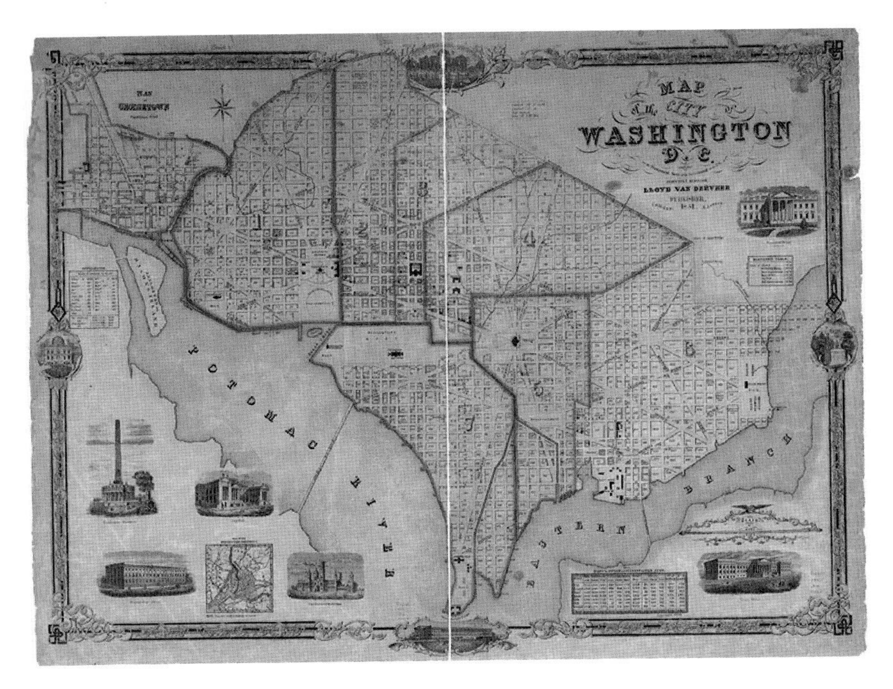

Map of the city of Washington, 1851. *Lloyd Van Derveer, Camden, N.J.*

the Eastern Branch and the Connogocheque." Some of the members of Congress cried out in protest; viewing this as a ploy by the president to make money from the foundation of the district. Washington and his family owned property in and near Alexandria, which was just seven miles upstream from Mount Vernon, Washington's home and plantation. These congressmen would only agree to an amendment to the original act that would allow Alexandria into the federal district if the new act contained a prohibition against building federal offices on the Virginia side of the Potomac River.

Eventually, the final site was just below the fall line of the Potomac, which was the farthest point upstream that oceangoing boats could navigate. It included several ports and became a key location for transferring goods, particularly tobacco, between ships and land and river transports. The only drawback to the site was that it was also accessible to the forces of foreign armies, as became apparent two decades later when British invaders burned the city during the War of 1812.

After the land was given to the government by the states of Maryland and Virginia, and the towns of Georgetown and Alexandria were included in the new district, the remainder of the territory was divided into Washington City, the county of Washington on the Maryland side of the Potomac (named after George Washington) and Alexandria County on the Virginia side.

This was not always a smooth process, however. Many of the landowners who were already present in what had become the district were justifiably angered at having their land taken away from them. One of the most prominent was David Burns, who owned 650 acres right in the heart of the district. He and a number of other landowners protested the creation of the district, and it would be months before they relented and signed an agreement with Washington to give up their farms. Burns and eighteen other men were compensated for land taken for public use. The remaining land could be sold for business, but half of it was given to the public.

Once the rest of these hurdles were cleared, Washington began appointing commissioners and planners to begin the actual creation of the district. Pierre Charles L'Enfant was appointed to devise the plan for the new city, a grid that would be centered on the United States Capitol and crossed by diagonal streets named for the states of the Union. L'Enfant's original plan was presented in August 1791, and in it he had carved grand circles and plazas at the intersections of the north–south and east–west streets. They were later to be named in honor of notable Americans. L'Enfant also laid out a wide "Grand Avenue" that was in the center of an area now occupied by the National Mall. He also designed a narrow road (Pennsylvania Avenue) to connect the "Federal House" to the "Presidential Palace," as he referred to the Capitol building and the White House in his plans.

L'Enfant would ultimately design the grid as far as Boundary Street, which would later be called Florida Avenue. He was fired by President Washington in 1792 due to numerous conflicts with the commissioners whom Washington had chosen to oversee the construction. Legend also has it that there was a final incident that so angered the president that he had L'Enfant fired on the spot. L'Enfant allegedly blew up a house that stood in his way with explosives! L'Enfant was said to have lured the reluctant owner outside and then had his men fill the house with gunpowder. It wasn't standing in the path of progress after that!

After L'Enfant's dismissal, Washington and the commissioners appointed surveyor Andrew Ellicott to complete the planning and the design of the capital. To the dismay of L'Enfant, Ellicott soon revised his predecessor's plans, straightening Massachusetts Avenue and eliminating several plazas and streets. Ellicott, unlike L'Enfant, had his plans engraved and published and they became the basis for future plans of the city. Washington's grid pattern consists of numbered streets running north–south and lettered streets running east–west. Strangely, there is no "J" Street. Popular legend has it that this was because of L'Enfant's personal dislike for John Jay, but the real story is not so colorful. It was really done to prevent the confusion that would result from the similarities in how the Roman numerals of "I" and "J" were written.

In 1800, the seat of government, which had been operating in other cities, was finally moved to Washington, and on February 27, 1801, the district was formally placed under the jurisdiction of Congress.

The city slowly grew in the years that followed and construction began on many of the major buildings. The entire district relied on Congress for support for capital improvements and economic development but funds were slow in coming. Congress lacked loyalty to the city's residents because they couldn't vote. The residents had nothing to offer the politicians, so the much-needed support went elsewhere. Because of this, the streets and health conditions of Washington lagged far behind other large cities in the country for many years.

After its first decade, however, Washington seemed to be coming into its own. It would be the War of 1812 that would strike the first blow against the fledging U.S. government. In 1814, President James Madison and the men of Congress were forced to flee the district before the approach of British troops. Between August 19 and August 29, British soldiers swept into the capital during what became the most destructive raid of the war. On August 24, they burned the most important public buildings, including the White House, the U.S. Capitol, the Arsenal, the Navy Yard, the Treasury, the War Office and the bridge across the Potomac. The American militia, which had collected at Bladensburg, Maryland, to protect the capital, retreated from Washington before it was destroyed.

The war ended in victory for the Americans but Washington was in ashes. It would take decades to rebuild the city, and construction would continue into the days of the Civil War. At that time, President Abraham Lincoln insisted that work on the U.S. Capitol building continue. Washington remained a small city of only a few thousand residents, virtually deserted during the sweltering heat of the summer, until the outbreak of the war in 1861. President Lincoln created the Army of the Potomac to defend the federal capital—only a short distance from the Confederate capital of Richmond, Virginia—and thousands of

U.S. Capitol building under construction. *National Archives.*

soldiers came to the area. The expansion of the federal government to administer the war, as well as its legacies such as veteran's pensions, turned Washington into a thriving city.

Slavery was abolished in the federal district in April 1862, eight months before Lincoln issued the Emancipation Proclamation. Slavery had been a controversial subject in Washington for nearly two decades before the Civil War and had been one of the factors that caused the city of Alexandria to leave the district and return to Virginia's jurisdiction. Alexandria had been a center for slave trading for many years, and with talk of abolition in the nation's capital, it chose to leave the district rather than suffer financially from a ban on slavery. Because of this, Alexandria County had retroceded back to Virginia in 1846.

Throughout the Civil War, the city was defended by a cluster of military forts that managed to deter the Confederates from most attacks. The notable exception was the Battle of Fort Stevens in July 1864 in which Federal soldiers repelled an assault under the command of Confederate General Jubal A. Early. This battle was the only time that a U.S. president came under enemy fire during wartime when Lincoln came to the fort to observe the fighting.

On April 14, 1865, just days after the end of the war, President Lincoln was shot in Ford's Theater by an assassin named John Wilkes Booth. He died the following morning in a house across the street from the theater and became the first American president to be murdered. This event, and the conspiracies that surrounded it, remains one of the most shocking events in the history of Washington.

In the latter part of the 1800s, Washington continued to change, grow and expand. In the early 1880s, the Washington Canal was finally filled in. The canal had originally been formed from Tiber Creek and it connected the Capitol with the Potomac, running along the north side of the Mall, where Constitution Avenue is today. As the nation moved from waterways to railroads as its leading mode of transportation, the canal slowly became a stagnant sewer. Many reformers blame the conditions of the canal for the rise in diseases and epidemics in the mid-1800s. Health officials breathed a sigh of relief when it was removed.

The Washington Monument, after four decades of construction, finally opened in 1888 and became the tallest building in the world at that time. Plans were made to further develop the monumental aspects of the city, and projects included work contributed by notables like Daniel Burnham, Frederick Law Olmsted and others. Development of the Lincoln Memorial and other structures on the National Mall appeared in the early 1900s, and new projects (along with the renovations of the originals) continue today.

Over the course of the last century, Washington has been rocked by scandals, assassination and unrest. It has seen the rise and fall of presidents and the public arrest of its mayor. There have been protests, sniper shootings, a terrorist attack and the creation of a reputation as "America's murder capital." The history of Washington is filled with deeds of the good, the just and the powerful, but it is also filled with the acts of those who stand on the shadowy side of the line between good and evil. For whatever reason— be it greed, a quest for power or a thirst for blood—these individuals have given Washington the designation of "wicked."

And these are the dark characters that we will be visiting in the pages ahead. Hold on, because at times it's going to be a bumpy ride!

1.

Politics Can Be Murder

The idea of a politician having a murderous streak must have begun with Alexander Hamilton. Even before his fateful duel with Aaron Burr, this member of the contingent of founding fathers had a penchant for bickering with just about everyone. He despised John Adams and actively disliked Thomas Jefferson and James Madison, but his hatred for Aaron Burr bordered on pathological. Although Hamilton and Burr maintained a superficial relationship, Hamilton seemed bent on destroying his "friend" politically from the time Burr was elected to the U.S. Senate in 1791, if not before then.

No one knows what originally caused the rift between Hamilton and Burr, although Hamilton always maintained that it was purely political. Others have suggested that a romantic rivalry may have existed between them, with both men competing for the same woman. It should be noted that Hamilton and Burr were both unapologetic adulterers. Hamilton even had an affair with his own sister-in-law and was forced to make a public account of another affair with a woman named Maria Reynolds.

Whatever the cause of Hamilton's hatred, he criticized Burr relentlessly. He was particularly cruel during the election of 1800, when Burr was running for president. (Burr lost by a handful of votes to Thomas Jefferson in one of the most contested presidential elections in history, and coming in second, he became vice president.)

For years, Burr ignored Hamilton's writings and caustic jibes, but that changed in 1804 when Burr was running for governor of New York. He suffered an embarrassing loss, mostly due to Hamilton's efforts against

Left: Alexander Hamilton. *Library of Congress.*

Right: Aaron Burr. *Library of Congress.*

him. During the campaign, a letter appeared in a newspaper that was unfriendly to Burr. Although it was not written by Hamilton, the letter noted, among other things, that Burr was "a dangerous man...who ought not to be trusted." When the letter writer, Dr. Charles D. Cooper, was challenged on this statement, he defended his position and stated: "I could detail to you a still more despicable opinion which General Hamilton has expressed of Mr. Burr."[2]

No one has ever learned what this "still more despicable opinion" that Hamilton may have expressed was, but some have ventured that he accused Burr of incest with his daughter. Whatever it might have been, Burr decided that it needed clarification, and he demanded that Hamilton provide it. Hamilton was evasive in his replies and refused to state what he allegedly told Dr. Cooper. More letters were exchanged between the two men, growing more heated with each passing day. Finally, their animosity led to what has become one of the most famous duels in American history.

On the hot morning of July 11, 1804, Aaron Burr, vice president of the United States, and Alexander Hamilton, one of the country's most eminent statesmen, faced one another with pistols on a stretch of land overlooking the Hudson River in Weehawken, New Jersey. Each man was seeking to kill or maim the other in what was referred to as "the court of last resort."

Hamilton had spent the previous evening preparing for his possible death at the hands of a superior marksman. He settled his affairs and penned letters that stated that he had no personal animosity toward Burr, only political. He concluded his letter: "I shall hazard much and can possibly gain nothing." This sentiment did not stop him from going to the field of honor with gun in hand the following day.

Perfect decorum was displayed at Weehawken. When Burr and his second saw Hamilton approaching the field with his own second, they stood straight, removed their hats and saluted in a gentlemanly manner. The seconds made the arrangements, measuring the distance between the combatants and carefully loaded the pistols. Then, Burr and Hamilton took their assigned places. At the moment of truth, Burr pulled the trigger. Hamilton lurched upward, spun to the left and fell on his face. When he hit the earth, his finger convulsively jerked the trigger and his pistol discharged into the air. The bullet clipped off a tree branch high over Burr's head.

While Hamilton bled into the earth (he died the following day), Burr was taken away from the site. He had survived the encounter and received the satisfaction that he sought. He paid the price for that satisfaction, however. He soon faced murder indictments in New York and New Jersey and faced the scorn of the nation, which was horrified by Hamilton's demise. Burr's political career was ruined, giving Hamilton in death what he had tried so hard to accomplish during his life.

The Code Duello

It comes as a surprise to many modern readers that eminent politicians like Burr and Hamilton would engage in such a bloody business, but their duel was hardly an isolated event. Deadly duels were frequently fought throughout the country—from before America's independence to well after the Civil War—by some of our most esteemed citizens. Future presidents, members of Congress, judges, governors and generals often found themselves on the field of honor, settling real and imagined attacks on their dignity. Both Burr and Hamilton had been involved in other duels, as had many politicians close to them. On one occasion, Hamilton had nearly dueled with future president James Monroe, but (ironically) Aaron Burr stepped in and helped to settle the situation.

Stephen Decatur. *Project Gutenberg*.

Dueling began in medieval Europe and became popular over the centuries, especially in Ireland, where it became a sport as well as a means of settling disputes. The Code Duello, developed there in 1777, became a set of rules that covered nearly every American duel and contained a list of provisions for all aspects of civilized combat. It outlined the exact number of steps to be measured between combatants, rules about cowardice, proper behavior and more.

Across the country Americans enthusiastically killed one another with style, and nowhere was this more true than at the Bladensburg Dueling Ground. This place, located just over the Maryland border from Washington, became known as "The Dark and Bloody Grounds." There were more than fifty duels fought here during the first half of the nineteenth century, but perhaps the most famous involved naval hero Stephen Decatur. The conqueror of the Barbary pirates was at the height

Bladensburg Dueling Grounds in the 1850s. *Harper's Weekly.*

of his national popularity when he was shot to death by a bitter fellow officer, James Barron, in 1820.

Barron's hatred of Decatur stretched back more than thirteen years. Barron had been in command of the frigate *Chesapeake* when it encountered the British ship *Leopold* off the coast of Virginia. Britain was then in the habit of boarding American ships and kidnapping sailors, claiming that they were British citizens. Barron's ship was so unprepared for defense that he decided to pull down his colors, submit his vessel to be searched and allow several of his men to be taken. All of this occurred without the firing of a single cannon! The encounter outraged America and became one of the events that led to the start of the War of 1812.

Barron was court-martialed and suspended from service after a humiliating process that was presided over by Stephen Decatur. Over the course of the next several years many lengthy and venomous letters were exchanged between the two men. After much arguing, Barron issued a challenge to Decatur that the two men meet on the field of honor. It seemed a one-sided battle. Decatur was known as an expert marksman and Barron was extremely nearsighted—a troublesome handicap when dueling. Pistols at eight paces were agreed upon with the additional provision, in deference to Barron's eyesight, that each man would take deliberate aim at the other before the count.

Barron, Decatur and their seconds met at the Bladensburg Dueling Ground on the morning of March 22, 1820. After they had taken up their positions, Barron spoke to Decatur: "Sir, I hope on meeting in the next world, we shall be better friends than in this." Decatur, who had told friends that he only intended to wound Barron, replied: "I have never been your enemy, sir."

After the call, shots rang out in a single thunderous noise and both men fell, crumpling to the ground at almost the same time. Each man believed that he was dying, and lying in pools of blood only a few feet away from one another, they spoke. Stephen Decatur said: "I am mortally wounded; at least I believe so. I wish that I had fallen in the service of my country." Making his peace, Barron begged for forgiveness. Decatur forgave him but "not those who have stimulated you to seek my life."

The two men were carried from the field. Decatur was returned to his Washington home and he died from his injury later on that night. Barron, however, survived the duel, but he had little reason to celebrate. Like Aaron Burr, he lived to face the anger of a country that was grieving over its fallen hero.

The earth of the Bladensburg Dueling Grounds tasted more than its share of blood. A year before the duel between Barron and Decatur, another fatal battle took place between General Armistead T. Mason, a former senator from Virginia, and his cousin, Colonel John M. M'Carty. Mason had questioned M'Carty's right to vote at the polls in Leesburg, Virginia, an insult that so enraged the other man that he immediately challenged Mason to a duel. However, his challenge set the terms and conditions for the fight, which went against the Code Duello. The code specifically stated that only the challenged party had the right to place conditions on the fight. On that note, Mason declined but informed his cousin that he would gladly accept if a proper dueling offer was extended.

M'Carty ignored him and painted Mason as a coward. Mason now challenged M'Carty, but he was dismissed due to his earlier refusal to fight. Although seething with anger, Mason took the advice of friends and let the matter drop—until a future U.S. president convinced him to take up the matter again.

Andrew Jackson, a man who had spilled blood in many duels, bluntly told Mason that he needed to challenge M'Carty again. Inspired by the man they called Old Hickory, Mason wrote a note to M'Carty and informed him that he had resigned his commission in order to be free to challenge and fight a duel. He dispatched his second with the note and offered to M'Carty that any distance and any weapons that he chose could be used in the duel. Once again, M'Carty refused, citing Mason's original cowardice. It was only when Mason's second threatened to slap him that M'Carty reluctantly agreed to the battle.

Whether he was inspired by Mason's determination for bloodshed or afraid of it, M'Carty proposed that they settle their differences once and for all by jumping off the dome of the U.S. Capitol. Mason's second rejected this as a violation of the code (and obviously insane) and then M'Carty proposed that they blow themselves up with a gunpowder keg. Finally, he withdrew his ridiculous suggestion and accepted a fight with muskets charged with buckshot, at a distance of ten feet. Mason's second, based on his friend's instructions of any distance and any weapon, was forced to accept. It was bound to be suicide for both men, but thanks to a friend, the conditions were modified to twelve feet with a single ball.

The two cousins met at the Bladensburg Dueling Grounds on the morning of February 6, 1819. Even though the grounds were blanketed with snow, M'Carty stripped to his shorts and rolled up his sleeves. Mason stood watching him in a heavy overcoat. They were presented with their weapons and warned not to fire before the count of three. With the muzzles of their weapons almost touching, the men fired at the same time. Mason fell dead, his aim apparently thrown off by his heavy coat. M'Carty's shoulder was shattered as Mason's ball entered his wrist and tore a path through his arm. He survived the duel but he lost the ability to use his right arm. In the years that followed, he never forgot that horrific, blood-soaked morning and he eventually lost his mind.

In spite of all of this, the seconds who were present that day were able to report that "the affair, although fatally, was honorably terminated."

Those same words could not be used to describe the pathetic 1836 duel that took place between two congressmen, Jesse Bynum of North Carolina and Daniel Jenifer of Maryland. Jenifer had denounced in the House what he felt was the poor course of President Jackson's party, which caused Bynum to leap to his feet and declare that it was ungentlemanly of Jenifer to say such words. Jenifer insisted that Bynum take back his words, but the other man refused. Minutes later, they were on their way to the Bladensburg Dueling Grounds, with fellow congressmen serving as seconds and witnesses.

Both men stood on the field, ten feet apart, and each boasted of what a fearsome marksman he was. The first shots were fired but neither man was hit. The pistols were reloaded three more times, but after the fourth volley of shots both men were still standing, unscathed.

Before the sixth shot, Bynum's pistol discharged, probably accidentally, and one of Jenifer's seconds prepared to shoot the man. This was a rigid rule in the Code Duello, stating that if a man fired early, his opponent's seconds had the right to shoot him down. But Jenifer ordered the man not to shoot, and he took aim himself, fired—and missed again! After six missed shots, the duel was, mercifully, called a draw.

More and more blood continued to be spilled on the Bladensburg Dueling Grounds and public concern began to rise about the continuation of this legalized murder. Unfortunately, Maryland laws did not apply to the residents of Washington, so even if a law was passed to prohibit duels at Bladensburg, it would not have any effect on those who used the grounds with the most frequency. Then, finally, in 1838, an incident occurred that caused such a public outcry that Congress was forced to act.

A popular congressman from Maine named Jonathan Cilley was shot to death by another congressman, William Graves from Kentucky. Graves had been a stand-in for a New York newspaper editor named James W. Webb. Cilley had accused Webb of corruption, and Graves, a close friend of the editor, took exception to the accusation.

Graves, knowing weapons quite well, challenged the inexperienced Cilley to a duel. Cilley believed the whole thing foolish and never expected the duel to actually take place. But on the morning of the duel, he found himself at Bladensburg with a rifle in his hand. The two men took up positions eighty yards apart and both fired, but no one was struck.

The shots were repeated, and still no one was hit. The seconds reached an agreement that each man would receive one final round. If no one was hit this time, the duel would be declared a draw. The agreement proved fatal for Cilley. His leg was shot out from under him, cutting away an artery, and he died in a matter of seconds on the cold ground.

This fatal encounter caused a national uproar. The fallen congressman was young and left a wife and three small children behind. In the minds of many, Graves had killed him in cold blood. Newspapers called the duel "horrid and harrowing," and even former President Andrew Jackson, who had seen more than his fair share of blood and dueling, stated:

> *I cannot write on the murderous death of poor Cilley. If Congress does not do something to wipe out the state of the blood of murdered Cilley*

> *from its walls, it will raise a flame in the public mind against it, not easily to be quenched. Cilley was sacrificed.*[3]

And Jackson was right. Public outcry was strong after Cilley's funeral and it forced lawmakers to do something to appease it. The next session of Congress was forced to make dueling, or accepting or making a challenge, a criminal offense.

The law appeased the public, but it did not bring an end to the dueling. The challenges were declared in secret and the duelists met at Bladensburg under the cover of darkness for many years after dueling was declared illegal. It would not be until the Civil War before the "sport" of dueling would die out completely.

The Blood-Stained Halls of Congress

The first recorded physical clash between congressmen started over spit. In 1798, Representative Matthew Lyon of Vermont ran across the floor of the House and spit into the face of Connecticut's Roger Griswold. He did so because the Connecticut man had made fun of his Revolutionary War record. A resolution to expel "Spitting Lyon" didn't pass, but Griswold managed to get his own revenge.

Two weeks later, Griswold walked over to where Lyon was sitting and struck him over the head with a large hickory cane. Stunned and bleeding, Lyon managed to get to his feet, grabbed some fire tongs and began swinging back at his attacker. They tumbled on the floor, swung, scratched and pummeled one another for a few minutes before this undignified mêlée could be broken up. The two men signed a pledge the next day, promising not to commit any act of violence toward one another again.

This battle ended peacefully, but there is no denying that a precedent had been set.

The practice of dueling eventually fell from favor as a means of settling disputes (and became illegal after Congressman Graves killed fellow legislator Jonathan Cilley in 1838), but the U.S. Capitol still remained a very violent place. This was especially true during the years leading up to the Civil War, when differences over slavery and state's rights intensified to a dangerous level. Legislation was sometimes ended for the day over what amounted to nothing more than a murderous look exchanged between

Left: Ill-fated Senator Charles Sumner. *Library of Congress.*

Below: A contemporary drawing of the attack on Sumner. *Congressional Globe, 1856.*

two opposing lawmakers. Congress was often described as "seething like a boiling cauldron" and it was an often stated fact that every man on the floor of both Houses was armed with a revolver. James Hammond of South Carolina added that some men carried "two revolvers and a Bowie knife." Senator Benjamin Wade walked about with a sawed-off shotgun draped over his arm. One day, a pistol that was concealed in one House member's desk went off, causing quite a disturbance. Representative William Holman of Indiana, who was present that day, recalled that after the weapon discharged, "there were fully thirty or forty pistols in the air."

Without a doubt, the most disturbing incident from those troubled times was the brutal beating of Massachusetts Senator Charles Sumner. On May 19, 1856, the ardent abolitionist delivered his famous "Crimes Against Kansas" speech, in which he harshly criticized the efforts of Southerners to force slavery into the territory. Sumner's speech was overwrought with fiery rhetoric and took a number of sharp digs at Andrew Pickens Butler, a pro-slavery senator from South Carolina. At one point in the speech, Sumner referred to Butler as one of slavery's "maddest zealots." He also went on to refer to slavery as Butler's "harlot," which was "polluted in the sight of the world, is chaste in his sight."

Butler would have been angry, and even justified in striking Sumner, if he had been present in the Senate chamber to hear the speech. He had not heard it, but a relative and fellow Carolina representative, Preston S. Brooks, was there and he was enraged over Sumner's insults.

Three days later, Brooks quietly entered the Senate chamber and found Sumner working at his desk. He cleared his throat and when he had Sumner's full attention, he announced to him: "I have read your speech twice over carefully. It is a libel on South Carolina and Mr. Butler, who is a relative of mine."

Then, without any sort of warning, Brooks produced a heavy cane and began pummeling Sumner over the head with it! He beat the man until the cane splintered and the Massachusetts man was on the floor in a pool of blood.

People in the North reacted to the assault with horror, but in the South, Brooks was hailed as a hero. Southerners sent him commemorative canes with the words "hit him again" inscribed on them. The event was later seen as an ugly foreshadowing of the Civil War to come.

Sumner's injuries kept him out of the Senate for three years, and his empty chair was displayed as a symbol for the abolitionist movement. Several weeks after the attack, a House investigation committee concluded that it was a breach of congressional privilege. The report stated that it was an aggravated assault on not only Senator Sumner, but on the right to freedom of speech itself. Debate raged in the House over whether or not to dispel Brooks, but eventually he decided to resign on his own. But he did not stay away for long. He ran for office again and was sworn in just two weeks after his resignation.

Ironically, Brooks died five months later from liver disease. His victim, Charles Sumner, returned from his convalescence and served in the Senate until 1874.

Not all of the murderous attacks at the Capitol involved one congressman attacking another. One of them actually involved a former politician and the newspaperman who had effectively ruined his career. The congressman, William Preston Taulbee, saw his destruction in a single headline: "Kentucky's Silver-Tongued Taulbee Caught in Flagrante, or Thereabouts, with Brown-Haired Miss Dodge."

The story beneath the headline was written by another Kentuckian, Charles Kincade, Washington correspondent for the *Louisville Times*. While the facts of the scandal are still being argued today, Taulbee chose not to run for re-election after the story had broken. Instead, he did what many other former lawmakers have done—he became a lobbyist.

Since this career choice continued to bring Taulbee to Capitol Hill, it's not surprising that the former congressman and the newspaper writer frequently ran into one another. Each considered the other man to be ungentlemanly and beneath contempt. Taulbee frequently insulted Kincade in the corridors of the Capitol, and occasionally would reach over and snatch the reporter's nose or one of his ears, giving it a sharp tug. According to custom, this meant that Taulbee did not consider Kincade "man enough" to be worthy of fighting.

On February 28, 1890, Taulbee and Kincade met for the last time on a set of marble stairs leading up to the House of Representatives press gallery. Earlier that day, Taulbee had entered the House chamber and he and Kincade had exchanged insults. Taulbee could have easily overpowered the reporter, who was barely five feet tall, weighed less than one hundred pounds and was in poor health. Instead, the burly lobbyist humiliated him by tossing him around by the collar and laughing at him.

Kincade left and went home for a pistol.

Around 1:30 p.m., Taulbee and a friend went down the marble stairs for lunch in the House dining room. The staircase is in a "Y" shape—twin staircases from the second floor to a landing, with a single flight leading down from the landing to the first floor. Taulbee and his friend came down one staircase and Kincade took the other. The reporter caught up to them just below the landing.

"Can you see me now?" Kincade reportedly asked the former congressman.

As Taulbee turned toward Kincade, his friend (perhaps catching a glimpse of Kincade's pistol) fled back up the stairs. Before Taulbee could answer the reporter's strange query, Kincade fired. The bullet struck Taulbee in the face, just below his eye. He collapsed onto the steps, blood already pooling beneath him. Moments later, a policeman rushed to the scene and demanded to know what had happened.

Kincade was still standing on the steps, his pistol dangling from his fingers. He spoke softly to the policeman and said: "I did it."

The former congressman was rushed from the scene and taken to Providence Hospital. He clung stubbornly to life for almost two weeks before succumbing to his wounds at the age of thirty-nine.

Kincade was tried for murder but the jury ruled that he had acted in self-defense and he was set free. He died in Cincinnati in 1906 while working as a reporter.

To this day, a stain remains on the marble stairs at the exact place where William Taulbee was shot. Legend has it that it is a stain that was left behind by the former congressman's blood. Merely a legend? Perhaps—although some of the older guards and maintenance workers at the Capitol will tell you that no cleaning agent has ever been able to remove that stain. It endures, leaving a lasting mark on the sometimes dark history of Capitol Hill.

One strange congressional incident did not end in death but it did include the attempted murder of a senator, right in the Senate chamber. On May 29-30, 1908, a Wisconsin senator named Robert M. Lafollette was leading a filibuster against the Aldrich-Vreeland bill. The bill was perfectly legitimate and was designed to allow the United States currency to expand during times of panic. For some reason, Lafollette was violently opposed to it. Little did he know, however, that there were men who were just as adamant about seeing it passed.

Lafollette began his filibuster—a method used by lawmakers that allows them to talk about anything that they want in order to prevent a vote on a bill they do not like—at 12:20 p.m. on the afternoon of May 29.

Lafollette continued for hour after hour. The rule of a filibuster is that you must remain talking and you cannot leave the Senate floor. As evening approached, the senator requested "energy drinks" of milk and raw eggs to be brought to him every so often from the Senate dining room.

At some point between 10:00 p.m. and 11:00 p.m., he received another of these mixtures and he began to drink it. Suddenly, his face took on a sour expression and he started to choke. He put the glass down immediately and it occurred to him that someone was trying to poison him. Lafollette was sure that one of his many enemies had decided to get rid of him. The senator had a reputation for being a man who could not be bought. Were they trying to kill him instead?

A few minutes later, Lafollette, still leading the filibuster, began to feel nauseated. His symptoms quickly got worse. His stomach churned, his bowels roiled and shooting pains stabbed his abdomen. Although hunched over and wincing in pain, Lafollette refused to leave the Senate. Heroically, he stayed on for another half dozen hours. Finally, he surrendered at exactly 7:03 in the morning.

Lafollette had continued talking for sixteen hours and forty-three minutes—the longest filibuster in history at that time. Unfortunately, it was not long enough. Later on that day, the Aldrich-Vreeland bill was passed.

A short time later, a laboratory reported on the mixture that made the senator sick. According to the chemical analysis, the egg and milk drink also contained a poison called ptomaine—and there was enough in it to kill a man. Someone had tried to kill a filibuster by murdering the senator who started it. The figurative phrase that had been used up until that point, "kill a filibuster," took on a haunting, literal meaning.

2.

Legally Insane

Murder and Daniel Sickles

Murder has always been enough of a commonplace occurrence in Washington that it's rare when a single homicide attracts much attention—unless that homicide involves a well-known congressman, a famous composer's son and an attempted cover-up by the president of the United States. With those elements combined, it's no wonder that Washington society was stunned in February 1859 when they heard of a murder that occurred in wealthy Lafayette Square.

The scandalous event involved Representative Daniel Sickles of New York and his friend, Phillip Barton Key, the son of "Star-Spangled Banner" composer Francis Scott Key. Sickles murdered Key in broad daylight, practically in front of the White House, with a number of witnesses present. But thanks to some help from President James Buchanan and the new legal defense of "temporary insanity," he got away with it.

Sickles was well-known in Washington. He was married to the beautiful daughter of an Italian music teacher, and Theresa Sickles was described as being charming and well-educated, along with being very attractive. After his marriage, Sickles worked in London for the Foreign Service for a short time and then was involved in the election campaign of President James Buchanan. He and his wife moved into their home on Lafayette Square and became a major part of Washington's elite society. Twice weekly they entertained the influential of Washington and the house became the center of both social and political circles.

Sickles later succeeded in winning back his congressional seat in New York and this caused him to start spending a lot of time away from home,

General Daniel Sickles after losing his leg at Gettysburg. *Library of Congress.*

leaving his wife, who had been just seventeen when they married, to fend for herself. While Sickles was away, Theresa began being spotted in the company of handsome widower Phillip Barton Key.

Everyone in Washington was soon talking about the affair, which was not carried out very discreetly. Key even rented his own house in Lafayette Square, just a block away from the Sickles home, so that they could get together as often as they liked. Rumor had it that they met at least three times each day. Key would stand in the park in front of Theresa's home and wave his handkerchief at her whenever he wanted to meet.

Sickles missed all of the signs of the affair, which had started on a sofa in his own parlor. Meanwhile, Key grew even bolder, ignoring warnings of violence that could result if the affair was found out. He boasted that he carried a weapon in his pocket, just in case.

Gossip about an improper relationship between Theresa and Key eventually made its way to Sickle, but it was an anonymous note that convinced him of the affair. The note, which had been slipped under his door read, in part: "I do assure you, [Key] has as much use of your wife as you have."[4] Sickles investigated and found that the allegations were true. According to House clerk George Woodridge, the revelation "unmanned him completely." The congressman's "exhibitions of grief" were so violent that Woodridge assisted him in retreating to a private room near the House chamber to avoid a public scene.

Sickles was enraged and distraught over the affair. He went home and confronted Theresa with what he knew. That same evening she wrote a long and detailed confession, which was very explicit for those prudish times. She implored her husband to "spare her," which Sickles did, but only after she signed the confession in front of two witnesses. That night, Theresa slept on the floor of her friend Octavia's room, while Sickles stayed in the bedroom. Servants later told of hearing sobbing coming from both bedrooms that night.

Sickles told a friend the next day: "I am a dishonored and ruined man."

The next morning, Phillip Key, not realizing that the affair had been found out, walked past the Sickles house and waved his handkerchief at the window. When Theresa failed to respond to his signal, he left, but came back and tried again later on in the day. On his third trip to the park, Key was met by the Sickles' dog, which ran out of the house when he saw him. Key made a show of playing with the dog, waving his handkerchief the entire time.

Sickles, however, had seen the less than subtle signals and shouted at George Woodridge and another visitor, Samuel Butterworth: "That villain has just passed my house!" Butterworth tried to placate his friend, arguing that a public scene would only provide more gossip about the affair. Sickles brushed him off, stating that the whole town knew of it anyway. By now, the congressman was well past reason and hardly concerned about appearances.

Arming himself with two derringers, Sickles rushed out of the house and into the park. He screamed at Key: "Key, you scoundrel! You have dishonored my house—you must die!"

As Key thrust his hand into his jacket, Sickles fired, but the shot only grazed the other man. Sickles raised his hand to fire again and Key grabbed him by the collar of his coat. As they struggled, the gun fell to the ground. Sickles pulled away from him and drew the second gun.

Key pleaded with him: "Don't murder me!" Then, he threw a pair of opera glasses at Sickles in a desperate attempt to ward off his attacker.

Sickles was undeterred and fired again. This time, the bullet struck Key, penetrating near his groin. Key murmured that he was shot and collapsed against a tree. Sickles stood over him and pulled the trigger again. The gun misfired. As Key cried in desperation, Sickles calmly reloaded the derringer and pressed it close to his former friend's chest. He fired again and this time, the shot was fatal. Even so, Sickles was still not finished. He placed the muzzle against Key's head, and again pulled the trigger. It misfired again and he stepped away.

Thomas Martin, a Treasury Department clerk, had witnessed the murder and he ran to the scene. Sickles turned to him and asked: "Is the scoundrel dead?"

Several men picked up Key's body and carried him to a nearby house, where he died a short time later. As he watched them go, Sickles stood at the edge of the park and mumbled the same phrase over and over again: "He violated my bed."

Sickles turned himself into the authorities immediately after the murder. At about the same time, President Buchanan received news about the incident from a young page, J.H.W. Bonitz, who had witnessed it. After hearing the report, Buchanan lied to Bonitz to try and protect his friend. He told the page that he should get out of town right away. Otherwise, he might be jailed and held without bond as a witness to the crime. Apparently, the president was unaware that others had witnessed the murder too, but his tactic worked on Bonitz. The page took some money that was offered to him by Buchanan and left Washington on the first train.

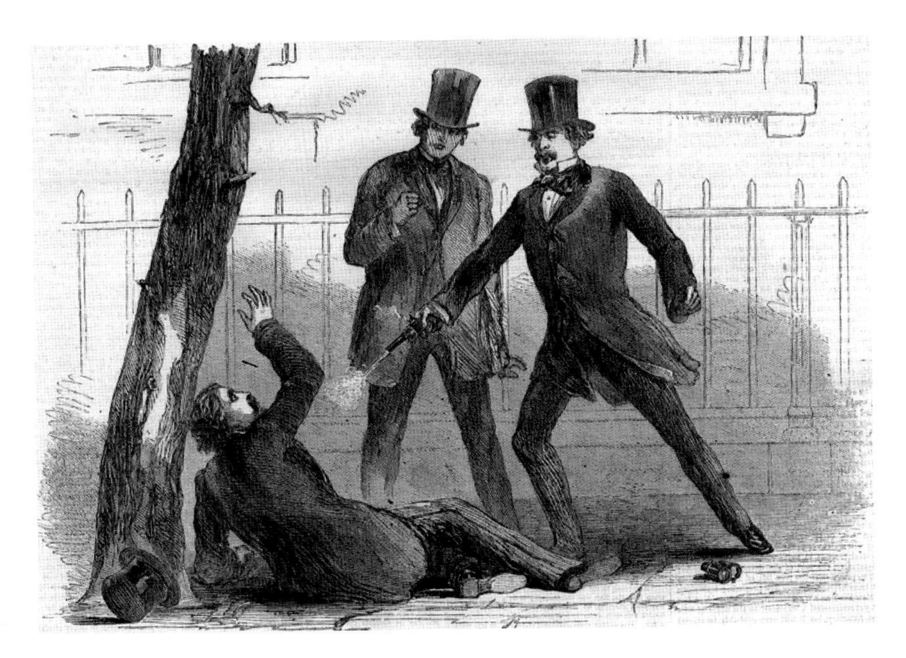

The murder of Phillip Barton Key. Harper's Weekly.

Before he was taken to jail, Sickles was permitted to make a short visit to his home. A large crowd was gathered outside, hoping for a glimpse of the famous killer. He was escorted inside and he found Theresa lying on the bedroom floor, stricken with grief. He uttered only once sentence to her before he left: "I've killed him."

News of the murder spread throughout the city and dominated newspaper headlines for days to come. Editorials were written that inflated the importance of the killing, stating that it reflected the moral decay of society in general, and more specifically, the increasing lawless conditions of Washington.

Sickles was indicted for murder and his trial was a spectacular one. He hired eight of the nation's most prestigious lawyers to defend him, while the prosecution was hampered from the beginning. Robert Ould, who was appointed by President Buchanan to replace Phillip Key as Washington's district attorney, was an inexperienced lawyer and incapable of handling such a complicated case. Despite pleas from the Key family (the president was still trying to help Sickles), Buchanan refused to replace him.

The trial began on April 4, 1859. The courtroom was crammed with curious spectators, and people outside peered in the windows hoping to catch a look at the proceedings. The case itself should have been simple. Sickles stalked and killed Key in an act of "remorseless revenge" and had done the deed in the open with plenty of people watching. He was obviously guilty of the crime with which he had been charged.

But the defense complicated the case by arguing that Sickles had been temporarily insane at the time of the murder, and that Key's defilement of his wife had made him that way. The insanity defense had been well-established in American courtrooms, but at that time there was no precedent for what the defense called an "irresistible impulse." Sickles, his counsel attested, had acted in a "transport of frenzy" that was fleeting in nature. He could not resist this impulse and acted in a manner that could not be stopped. For this reason, they said, he was not guilty of the crime.

The jury agreed, and after deliberating for less than an hour, Sickles was acquitted.

The verdict was followed by a spontaneous celebration in the streets of Washington, including a parade that was led by the U.S. Marine Band. Sickles was not exactly proclaimed a hero, but his actions were certainly understood by most. They believed that Sickles had a right to stand up for his honor, and one of the jurors in his trial, William Hopkins, even told newspapers: "I would not have been satisfied with a derringer or a revolver, but would have brought a howitzer to bear on the seducer."[5]

Sickles had been grievously wronged and the public was prepared to welcome him back to his proper place in society. But then Sickles did the unthinkable—he reconciled with his wife.

All of the goodwill that had followed the trial suddenly vanished and the public was in an uproar. Newspapers turned against him, as did many of his friends. Sickles was not ruined by the murder, but for forgiving his wife. Public reaction was so angry that Sickles was compelled to justify himself in a lengthy newspaper statement that was reprinted all over the country. In the letter, he made no apologies for murdering Key and for taking back Theresa. Instead, he appealed for the right to conduct his personal family life in private.

The open letter did little good. Sickles was considered a joke and was ostracized by his fellow members of Congress. Despised and the object of ridicule, Sickles decided not to run for re-election. But his colorful career was far from over.

When the Civil War began, Sickles raised a contingent of men from New York and organized them for battle. His patriotism so impressed President Lincoln that he assured Sickles a position after the war. He managed to wrangle a commission and rose to the rank of major general. At Gettysburg, Sickles continued his controversial career by gloriously disobeying orders. He decided to move his corps forward from its assigned position in General Meade's "fish-hook" across the battlefield. This jeopardized the entire Union line at the same time that Longstreet's Confederates were moving to attack the very place that Sickles had been ordered to hold.

During the battle, Sickles's right leg was hit and horribly mangled by a cannonball. On his way to the field hospital, where the leg would be amputated, Sickles calmly sipped wine and smoked a cigar. The wound ended his active service but he displayed the stump of his leg as a sign of his valor and heroism. In fact, he was so proud of his wound that he donated the shattered leg to the Army's National Medical Museum, where it remains on display today. For years after, he visited the leg on the anniversary of its removal.

When the war ended, President Andrew Johnson kept Lincoln's promise to find Sickles a position in government and appointed him military governor over the Carolinas during Reconstruction. Sickles described his new position: "I am a sort of Sultan, a sort of Roman consul. I was not only the military commander, I was the Governor of these two states; I was the Court of Chancery of these two states. I was a sort of Poobah."[6]

President Johnson found him to be a little too full of himself and relieved him of his duties in 1867.

That same year saw the death of Theresa Sickles at age thirty-one. General Sickles remarried four years later to Carolina Creash, whom he had met while serving as the American minister to Spain. He apparently made some waves in this position too, for he earned the nickname of the "Yankee King of Spain." He was forced to resign in 1873, but not before reportedly carrying on a steamy affair with the deposed Queen Isabella II.

Not surprisingly, his second marriage was a disaster and he and his wife were estranged for almost thirty years when she refused to return with him to the United States. Sickles managed to stay busy, however, serving another term in Congress and taking on a maid as his mistress. He was said to still be chasing women well into his nineties, and he died of natural causes in 1914.

3.

Washington's Greatest Conspiracy

The Assassination of Abraham Lincoln

Abraham Lincoln is considered today to be one of the most revered of all American presidents. During his lifetime, though, he was one of the most reviled. He was elected to the presidency during one of the most volatile periods in our nation's history and managed to win the election by a narrow margin.

When he left Springfield, Illinois, to come to Washington and begin his service to the country, Lincoln was one of the most hated men in America.

Lincoln's life was already in danger when he stepped aboard the train in Illinois. His mail had started to contain hate letters and death threats. Washington was crawling with rumors that Lincoln was going to be assassinated when he arrived. Reports came to General Winfield Scott that Southern rebels planned to seize Washington, block Lincoln's election and kill him. There was also the danger that someone might kill Lincoln during his trip east. The worst danger seemed to be in Baltimore, where gangs of men were calling for Lincoln's head. The threats were starting to be taken very seriously by the men who vowed to protect the new president, and William Seward, Lincoln's new secretary of state, and General Scott took great care in mapping out Lincoln's train route across America's turbulent landscape.

Lincoln's family joined him for the twelve-day journey to Washington, boarding the train in Indianapolis. Unfortunately, not even the presence of his wife and children prevented disaster from almost striking several times. One assassination attempt was averted when guards discovered a grenade in a satchel near the president's seat.

Abraham Lincoln. *Library of Congress.*

The train traveled across the country to New York, where newspapers and critics mocked Lincoln's awkward gestures and western mannerisms, and then south through New Jersey to Philadelphia. The family checked into the Continental Hotel, where the nearly exhausted Lincoln surrendered to another crowded and noisy reception. Late that evening, Chicagoan and friend Norman Judd called Lincoln to his rooms for a secret meeting with Allan Pinkerton, another Chicagoan and the head of the detective agency who now worked for the Philadelphia, Wilmington and Baltimore Railroad. A short, bewhiskered man with a Scottish burr, Pinkerton informed Lincoln that his detectives had uncovered a well-organized plot to assassinate the president-elect in Baltimore, a rabid secessionist city. Lincoln was scheduled to change trains there and the plotters intended to kill him as he took a carriage from one station to another. Pinkerton and Judd insisted that Lincoln foil the plot by leaving for Washington that night.

But the stubborn frontiersman refused, pointing out that he had promised to speak at Independence Hall the next morning and in Harrisburg the following afternoon. Still, if they really believed that he was in danger, he would try to get away from Harrisburg in the evening. He would not alter his plans completely. Lincoln then retired to his room to try and rest.

No sooner had he fallen into bed than a knock came at the door. It was William Seward's son, Frederick, with a letter from the secretary of state and General Scott. The letter warned that there was definitely a plan to kill Lincoln in Baltimore and that he had to avoid the city at all costs. Frustrated, Lincoln realized that he had no choice but to heed the warnings and make plans to do something he hated to do—to sneak into Washington, terrified of being killed by his own people.

The next day, which was Washington's birthday, Lincoln spoke at Independence Hall and then departed for Harrisburg that afternoon. On the train, Judd took Lincoln aside and rehearsed a clandestine getaway plan that Judd had worked out with railway officials and trusted military officers. At dusk, a special train would spirit Lincoln back to Philadelphia, where he would be ushered in disguise aboard a sleeping coach. A night train would take it to Baltimore and then another would take it to Washington in secret. In the morning, the regular presidential train would go on to Baltimore as scheduled, with Judd and a military escort onboard to protect Lincoln's family and traveling companions.

Again, Lincoln hated the idea of sneaking into Washington but decided to "run no risk where no risk was required," and he went along with Judd's scheme. The only demand that Lincoln made was that Mary be told of the plan. She learned of it that afternoon and was understandably upset. She considered it her right and duty to travel with the president and to stand by his side in case of danger. She realized that she could not in this case, but tearfully demanded that Lincoln's close friend Ward Hill Lamon accompany her husband. Mary knew that she could count on Lamon to protect Lincoln with his life.

That night, disguised in a large hat and an overcoat, Lincoln waited for the train in a carriage in Philadelphia. Lamon waited with him, armed with two revolvers, two derringers and two large knives. A Pinkerton agent arrived and escorted him to the train. The sleeping car, which was much too short for the gangly Lincoln, was reserved under a false name, supposedly for an invalid who was being accompanied by his sister. The "sister" was in reality a Pinkerton agent named Kate Warne. It was an inauspicious arrival into Washington, but at least Lincoln was safe and alive.

Lincoln reached the capital at dawn on February 23 and went straight to the Willard Hotel. He had not slept at all and his first view of Washington as the president-elect could not have cheered his heart. Looking out over the city from the carriage in which he rode, he saw only scenes of cold desolation. Down on the bank of the dirty Potomac River, he saw a white shaft of marble against the horizon. It was the unfinished monument to Washington, which looked toward the uncompleted dome of the Capitol Building. Scaffolds covered the cupola and cranes stretched over the dome. There were stacks of building material all around the Capitol and the unfinished Treasury Building. Washington was filthier than Lincoln remembered, with stinking livery stables and rancid saloons at every corner. Pigs rooted in the dirt streets off Pennsylvania Avenue and sewage swamps lay just steps away from the White House. Not far away, near land strewn with garbage, was an open drainage ditch "floating with dead cats and all kinds of putridity," wrote one visitor, "and reeking with pestilential odors." Even now, in the early morning hours, Lincoln noted the foul reek that hung over the city. It was the worst that Lincoln could recall.

Lincoln soon arrived at the hotel, a castle-like structure that boasted of running water in every room, and he checked into a suite, where he and his family would stay until the inauguration. Inside, Lincoln found a letter waiting for him: "If you don't resign, we are going to put a spider in your dumpling and play the Devil with you." This statement was followed by lines of obscene abuse and ended with "you are nothing but a goddamn Black nigger."

Mary arrived with the boys that afternoon, still shaken from her ordeal in Baltimore, where frenzied crowds had greeted the presidential train and had shouted for Lincoln. No violence had broken out but Mary had been terrified. She collapsed at the hotel with one of her legendary headaches and did not stir again until late in the evening.

The opposition press noted with sarcasm that the Republican president had arrived without fanfare. And when details of the secret arrival leaked out, papers of all persuasion mocked Lincoln without mercy and published scathing cartoons about the "flight of Abraham." It was the beginning of a merciless smear campaign against the "backwoods president" and his "boorish" wife. Their taunts about his crude behavior and illiterate education wounded Lincoln badly, but he never replied to journalistic abuse, writing it off as part of the job.

Inaugural week was a nightmare for Lincoln. For one thing, the rabid and persistent office seekers refused to leave him alone, and in addition, the endless delegations from the office of outgoing president James Buchanan and his cabinet filed in and out of his hotel suite. Lincoln was also plagued by groups of congressmen and senators who harassed him about his cabinet choices and his policy of dealing with the South.

There were delegations from Virginia and the border states as well. One group came from the Virginia secession convention, wanting to see what Lincoln would do and whether they should secede or adjourn. The Virginians urged Lincoln to give them a "message of peace" to take home with them but he would only say that Southerners would be protected in all of their legal rights. Another delegation, consisting of border state Union loyalists, told Lincoln that he must avoid coercion at all costs. He must evacuate Fort Sumter, whose Union flag aggravated the situation with the secessionists, and he must offer "satisfactory guarantees" to the eight slave states still loyal to the Union. Seward had assured the border Unionists that the crisis would disappear within sixty days of Lincoln being in office, but the delegation now wanted assurances from Lincoln himself. Lincoln was blunt with them. He would, he told them, support a slave amendment for loyal states in the Constitution but he would never guarantee slavery in the territories. He also refused to give up any of the military forts the Union held in the South, but unknown to the border delegation, he did make an offer to the group from Virginia. He told them that if they could persuade the Virginia secession convention to disband, he would give up Fort Sumter. But the Virginians refused his proposal. All they could promise was devotion to the Union, and so both groups departed with no solutions in sight.

Somehow, in the midst of all of the commotion that week, Lincoln managed to complete his cabinet, even with rival factions harassing him down to the last appointment. It was during this time that Lincoln

William Seward. *National Archives.*

had his first problem with William Seward. After Lincoln ignored his suggestion for the appointment of postmaster general, Seward submitted his resignation on the eve of the inauguration. Lincoln was unsettled and realized that Seward, believing himself to be a greater politician than the new president, hoped to try and gain control over the cabinet and the administration itself. He reasoned that Lincoln, unable to do without Seward's superior abilities, would offer to remove his choice from the cabinet and replace him with the man his secretary of state wanted. But Lincoln told his assistant, John Nicolay, that he couldn't "afford to let Seward take the first trick" in their struggle for administrative leadership. Lincoln soon had a confidential chat with Seward and hinted that he might appoint someone else to take his place. Seward quickly withdrew his resignation and Lincoln took "the first trick."

Regardless, the two continued to clash. As Inauguration Day approached, Lincoln carefully crafted his speech. There was much at stake, and Lincoln polished and rewrote with great care. On March 3, he asked Seward to look it over and he returned with the advice that Lincoln should offer greater concessions to the South. He insisted also that Lincoln remove one offensive sentence, which stated that he would recapture all of the federal forts and arsenals that the rebels had already taken over. Lincoln had long been arguing that this needed to be done, but Seward convinced him to cut it so that he did not alienate the Southern Unionists, on whom much depended. Lincoln did so, but he would not concede much else. In his mind, the future of freedom depended on him standing firm. He had been freely and fairly elected and had not lied in any of his pledges to the people who voted for him and his party. If the Southerners did not like him, they were free to vote him out of office in 1864. But they had no right to separate the Union and he was not going to let them. The Union was the authority of the land and could not be wrecked by some disaffected minority. The principle behind secession was one of destruction, and no government had ever been established that allowed for its own demise. Lincoln was not going to stand by and watch the destruction of the government he loved.

The day of the inauguration was a grim one in Washington. Heavy storm clouds hung low in the sky and soldiers marched through the crowded streets of the city, ever watchful for the trouble that some said was coming. There were assassination rumors still in the wind, and for all of those who feared for Lincoln's safety, there were many others who hoped for terror to strike.

That morning, Lincoln stayed in his suite at the Willard Hotel. He read his inaugural address to his family and then asked to be alone for awhile. When the clock chimed noon, he dressed in a new black suit and stovepipe hat and departed for the lobby. President Buchanan called on him for the traditional carriage ride to Capitol Hill but the two men said little to one another during the journey. The clouds had lifted over Washington and the sun was now brightly shining over the grand parade of horse-drawn floats and military bands. Double files of cavalry rode along the flanks of the carriage and lines of infantrymen filed along behind. Hundreds of other officers had been deployed by General Scott throughout the crowd, guarding against assassination. They mingled with the sidewalk crowds and sharpshooters peered over rooftops on both sides of the avenue. As Lincoln looked out over the throng, his eyes landed on the soldiers and he was dismayed to ponder that it was as though the country was already at war.

The inauguration of Abraham Lincoln. Legend has it that John Wilkes Booth was in the crowds that day. *Library of Congress.*

The carriage pulled up to the Capitol steps and thousands of people surged about the East Plaza where an enormous platform extended from the building's east wing. Pinkerton detectives stood about, watching for any signs of trouble, and soldiers watched from the windows of the Capitol and from the rooftops of adjacent buildings. On a nearby hill, artillerymen manned a line of cannons, prepared to rake the streets with deadly fire at the first sign of assassins.

Lincoln filed out onto the giant platform with about three hundred dignitaries. With a brisk wind blowing, he stood at the podium and looked out over the sea of faces below. Then, he unrolled the manuscript that contained his speech, perched a pair of steel-rimmed spectacles on his nose and began to read in a nervous but clear voice. He spoke at length to the concerns of the Southerners and assured them that he would not endanger their property, their peace or their personal security. He would not menace the institution of slavery as he had, according to the Constitution, no right to do so. But Lincoln also spoke about the supremacy of the national government and vowed to enforce federal law in all states. The Union was perpetual, he said, and could not be destroyed, and he promised to shed no blood in its defense unless forced to do so. He would, he vowed, "hold, occupy and possess" those southern forts still in Union possession.

Despite these proclamations to use whatever force necessary to save the Union, Lincoln went on to say:

> *We are not enemies, but friends. We must not be enemies. Though passion may have strained, it must not break our bonds of affection. The mystic chords of memory, stretching from every battlefield and patriot grave, to every living heart and hearthstone, all over this broad land, will yet swell the chorus of the Union, when again touched, as surely they will be, by the better angels of our nature.*

Lincoln then turned and faced Chief Justice Roger Brooke Taney and took his oath as the sixteenth president of the United States. Up on the hill, cannons fired into the wind and a cheer went up from the assembled crowd below. Lincoln had triumphed, it seemed, but little did he know that as his words echoed out over the audience that day, America was entering the most troubled period in its entire history. War was coming to Lincoln's very doorstep and the country was coming apart.

In the days, months and years that followed, the personality of Abraham Lincoln was altered considerably. Although he had long been prone to moodiness and "spells," his periods of reflection became longer and more pronounced. As the death toll of the war mounted on both sides, Lincoln became more and more obsessed with God and his divine plan for America—and for the president himself. Lincoln became convinced that he had been born to guide America through the War Between the States. His leadership during this period, although often questioned, never faltered, and the events of the early 1860s both strengthened and destroyed the man that Lincoln was.

The great loss of life and the bitter turmoil of the war took their toll on him. He changed and he became more bitter and dark. Gone was the humorous man who was apt to take off his shoes during staff meetings to "let his feet breathe." In his place was a sad, gloomy leader who was prone to severe depression. It was as if the weight of the entire nation had fallen on his shoulders. After bitter years of war and a hard-won re-election, however, the end to the bloodshed finally came.

On a cool Sunday evening, April 9, 1865, President Lincoln was returning home from a visit at the bedside of Secretary of State Stanton, who was recuperating from a broken jaw, when a messenger arrived with a telegram from General Grant. The end had come—the Confederate armies had surrendered! The Great War had finally ended and now Lincoln could only think of the best ways to repair the ties with the embattled and defeated South. He knew that the radicals in Congress would seek revenge against the Confederate states, but for now they were fearful of Lincoln's popularity with the voters. Lincoln knew that when things calmed down he had to have a policy of mercy solidified for the Union. He had to think carefully and coolly before he spoke to the crowds that formed outside of the White House on Monday evening, demanding a speech. When they stormed so loud outside of the windows that he could not deny them, he appeared for a moment, joking with them, putting them off and pretending to be unprepared. Finally, he slipped out of the situation by setting the band to strike up "Dixie."

The next night, Tuesday, the crowd returned, larger and more insistent than ever. Slowly, the president appeared on the steps, his face saddened by the loss of so many lives over the years. Sagely, he began to express quiet, merciful thoughts to those who crowded onto the White House lawn. He spoke of the joys of peace, saying nothing of punishment for the "rebels." He spoke of God and thanksgiving, not of vengeance. What had to be done was to get the Southerners back into the Union as tactfully as possible.

He told the assembled masses:

> *We all agree that the seceded states, so called, are out of their proper practical relation with the Union, and that the solid object of the government, civil and military, in regard to those states, is to again get them into that proper relation. I believe that it is not only possible, but in fact easier, to do this without deciding or even considering whether these states have ever been out of the Union, than with it. Finding themselves safely at home, it would be utterly immaterial whether they had ever been abroad.*

Edwin Stanton. *National Archives.*

These were the first words that Lincoln spoke concerning reconciliation with the former Confederacy, but they would not be the last. Over the three days that followed, peace and reconciliation "smoothed out the Mason and Dixon line."

Not surprisingly, Lincoln's mood was high and he felt exhilarated to know that the war had finally ended. He saw only good things on the horizon. But it would be Mary who saw a forewarning of doom. Lincoln and Mary were riding through the city on Friday afternoon, taking in the air before they arrived at the theater. She kept watching her husband, noting what now seemed to be his strange animation and unusual joyfulness. Evidently without thinking that he could be elated over the likely triumph of his policy of mercy, she was gripped with a sudden fear: "I have seen you thus only once before, it was just before our dear Willie died."

At the mention of his son's death, which had staggered him and haunted his dreams, Lincoln lost his cheerfulness and settled back into the same melancholy that had, since his youth, seemed "to drip from him as he walked." After a time, though, his spirits lifted somewhat, and by evening, when the curtain rose at the theater, he was optimistic once more.

Northerners, wanting life and laughter in the madness of victory, rushed to the theater to celebrate. It was Good Friday, which was usually a terrible night for theater owners, but it was a wondrous one in Washington of 1865. Ford's Theater was especially packed that night, for it had been announced that Lincoln planned to show himself in public. Everyone wanted to see the man who had guided the country so mysteriously to overwhelming success.

The theater was full to the doors as the curtain went up and the play began, but the audience gave only half its attention to the actors on the stage. They watched the president's empty box and waited for him to arrive.

When the Civil War ended, it did not end for everyone in Washington. There were many, in the North and the South, who refused to believe that the Confederacy had fallen.

One of these men was John Wilkes Booth, an actor who professed an undying devotion to the South. Booth was the son of Junius Brutus Booth, a professional actor. The elder Booth was considered by many to be so eccentric that he was nearly insane, a trait which father and son apparently shared. John Wilkes Booth was also the brother of Edwin Booth, perhaps the most famous stage actor of the period. Edwin often spoke of his brother's strangeness, and he would have had an even greater cause for concern had he known the dark secrets that his sibling hid in his heart.

While the war was still raging, Booth had been attempting to organize a paramilitary operation with a small group of conspirators. Their plan was to kidnap the president and take him to Richmond. After a number of failed attempts, it was clear that the plan would not work. Booth's hatred of Lincoln forced him to change his plans from kidnapping to murder. He did not explain to his confederates about this change until two hours before the event took place.

Booth had been a Southern sympathizer throughout the war. He was revered for his acting in the South, and during the war had been a spy and a smuggler, working with Southern agents in Maryland and Canada. He was also rabid in his pro-slavery views, believing that slavery was a "gift from God." He was convinced that Lincoln was a tyrant, and Booth hoped the murder of the president would plunge the North into chaos and allow the Confederacy to rally and seize control of Washington.

On the night of April 14, Booth stepped into Lincoln's box at Ford's Theater and shot the president in the back of the head. At the same time, another assassin tried to kill Secretary of State Seward. He was horribly scarred by a knife wound to the face, but survived. Secretary of War Edwin Stanton and General Grant were also slated to be killed, and presidential successor Andrew Johnson was only spared because of an assassin's cold feet. The shadow of a greater conspiracy hung over Washington and many questions have not been answered to this day, including whether Edwin Stanton was also involved in the assassination.

Some historians (and conspiracy theorists) believe that Stanton was one of the few to really gain by Lincoln's death. There was no question that Stanton had long been standing in Lincoln's shadow, so to speak, and was violently opposed to many of the president's policies. He favored a revenge policy of radical Reconstruction for the Southern states

John Wilkes Booth. *National Archives.*

and was enraged over Lincoln's gentle plans for rebuilding the South. Stanton would have gained even more power if the North had imposed a military occupation on the former Confederacy. Many believe that Stanton's behavior both before and after Lincoln's assassination raised many questions about his loyalty. For example: Stanton refused a request for Major Thomas Eckert to accompany Lincoln to Ford's Theater. The implication, according to some historians, was that Stanton knew something Lincoln didn't. Despite the many death threats Lincoln had received, Stanton only sent one bodyguard to the theater that night and this man abandoned his post to have a drink. He was never reprimanded for this. On the night of the assassination, telegraph lines in Washington, controlled by the War Department, mysteriously went dead, delaying the news of Booth's escape. Many believe this points to some sort of government conspiracy behind the murder. Booth's diary was given to Stanton after the assassination and it vanished for several years. When it was returned, eighteen pages were missing. A security chief would later testify that it had been intact when given to Stanton.

And there were other problems as well, although none of this would be brought to light until more than seventy years later! It was, of course, far too late by that time, but the mystery remains as to whether Stanton was in some way involved. Did he have a hand in Lincoln's death? We will never know, but there is no question that many other mysteries surrounding the Lincoln assassination remain unsolved.

The Lincoln party arrived at the theater and entered their reserved box, which had been adorned with drapes and Union flags, to the cheers of the crowd and to the musical strains of "Hail to the Chief." Onstage, the actors ceased their dialogue in deference to Lincoln. The play was a production called "Our American Cousin," presented by actress Laura Keene. It was a comedy, the sort of show that Lincoln liked best. The Lincolns were accompanied by a young couple, Major Henry Rathbone and his fiancée, Clara Harris. Lincoln slumped into a rocking chair that had been provided by the management to fit his long body and Mary was seated beside him, with Rathbone and Clara Harris to their right. Onstage, Harry Hawk, the male lead, ad-libbed a line: "This reminds me of a story, as Mr. Lincoln would say…" The audience roared and clapped and Lincoln smiled, whispering something to Mary. Behind him, the box door was closed but not locked, and in all of the excitement over the president's arrival, no one noticed the small peephole that had been dug out of it.

As the play progressed, guard John Parker left his post in the hallway outside of the box and either went down into the gallery to watch the play or left to have a drink. Those who believe there was a government conspiracy to kill Lincoln often point to John Parker as proof of it. Parker was Lincoln's only bodyguard that night and he had gone ahead to Ford's Theater that evening rather than accompany the president to the venue. A patrolman on the Washington police force, Parker was a lazy drunk with an appalling history of insubordination and insufficiency. He was totally unsuitable to guard the president and it is believed that if Ward Hill Lamon had been aware of the posting, he would have never allowed himself to be removed from the detail that night.

Onstage, the players hammed it up in silly and melodramatic scenes, and laughter rolled through the audience. As the Lincolns picked up the story, Hawk was a homespun American woodsman named Asa Trenchard and Laura Keene, a stunning actress with thick auburn hair, was his young English cousin, Florence Trenchard. A scheming English matron named Mrs. Mountchessington, convinced that Asa was a rich Yankee, was out to snare him for her daughter, Augusta. Lincoln chuckled along with the play, trying to keep his mind off of the troubles that lay ahead. Mary rested her hand on his knee and called his attention to situations on the stage, applauding happily at the funniest scenes. One of the actresses noted that while Lincoln never clapped, he did laugh "heartily" from time to time.

Meanwhile, John Wilkes Booth had been lurking about the theater all evening and finally approached the state box where the Lincolns and their guests were seated. He showed a card to an attendant and gained access to the outer door, which he found to be unattended. This should have been completely unexpected, but Booth was apparently not surprised by this development. As he slipped through the door and into the box, Booth jammed the door closed behind him. The laughter of the crowd concealed any noise that he might have made.

On stage, Mrs. Mountchessington finally discovered the shocking truth about Asa, that he was poor and no catch at all for her daughter. In stiff British rage, she sent Augusta to her room, reproached the American for his ill-mannered impertinence and then marched haughtily into the wings, leaving Asa alone on the stage.

During the evening, the Lincoln party had been discussing the Holy Land. The president made a comment about wanting to visit Jerusalem someday as he leaned forward and noticed General Ambrose Burnside in the audience of the theater. At that moment, Booth stepped forward. Major Rathbone stood from his seat to confront the intruder but before he could act, Booth raised a small pistol and fired it into the back of President Lincoln's head.

Rathbone seized the actor but Booth slashed him with a knife. Lincoln fell forward, striking his head on the rail of the box and slumping over. Mary took

A contemporary drawing of the assassination of President Lincoln. Harper's Weekly.

hold of him, believing him to have simply fallen, while Booth jumped from the edge of the balcony. His boot snagged on the bunting across the front of the box and he landed badly, fracturing his leg. As he struggled to his feet, he cried out "*Sic Semper Tyrannis*!" ("Thus it shall ever be for tyrants!") and he stumbled out of the theater using the back stage door. Both Rathbone and Clara Harris began to cry after him: "Stop that man! Stop that man!"

Clara pleaded once more: "Won't somebody stop that man? The president is shot!"

Her final scream snapped the audience out of its stunned stupor. Soon, voices began to take up the call of "Booth!" having recognized the famous actor as he plunged to the stage. In spite of this, however, he managed to easily escape from the close and crowded auditorium. Then, there were more screams, groans and the crashing of seats—but above it all came Mary Lincoln's shrill and terror-filled scream for her husband.

By now, the theater was in chaos. People were shoving into the aisles and rushing for the exits, with Laura Keene yelling at them from the stage: "For God's sake, have presence of mind and keep your places, and all will be well."

In the theater's audience was a young doctor named Charles Leale who rushed upstairs to Lincoln's aid. He fought his way into the president's box where a weeping Clara Harris tried to console Mary, who was holding Lincoln in the rocker and weeping hysterically. Leale laid the president on the floor and removed the blood clot from the wound to relieve the pressure on the brain. The bullet had struck him just behind the left ear, had traveled through the brain and lodged behind his right eye. Even this young doctor could see that the wound was a fatal one—the president was nearly dead. Lincoln's heart was barely beating but Leale reached into his mouth, opened his throat and applied artificial respiration in a desperate attempt to save him. A few moments later, Leale was joined by Dr. Charles Sabin Taft and the two men continued their efforts. They raised and lowered the president's arms while Leale massaged his chest, and then he forced his own breath into Lincoln's lungs again and again. At last, Lincoln was breathing on his own again, his heart beating with an irregular flutter. The president was failing—but he was still alive.

The two doctors, with some help from bystanders, managed to get the president out of Ford's Theater. Soldiers cleared a path through the crowd outside, where people rushed madly back and forth and milled about in confusion. A man named Henry Safford, who worked as a clerk at the War Department, beckoned to the doctors and they carried the president across the street into the Petersen house. Lincoln's unconscious form was laid in a small, shabby bedroom at the back of the house. His lanky frame was too long for the bed and they were forced to lay him down at an angle. Clara Harris and Major Rathbone, with his untreated arm bleeding profusely, brought Mary to the house. When she saw Lincoln in the back room, Mary ran to him, falling sobbing to her knees and calling him intimate names. She begged Lincoln to speak to her until finally the doctors led her to the front parlor, where she broke into convulsive weeping.

Help was summoned and soon Lincoln's aides and security men were attempting to try and calm the frenzy around them. Meanwhile, the surgeon general, Joseph K. Barnes, and Lincoln's own doctor, Robert Stone King, set to work on the president. They soon realized that it was no use—there was nothing that could be done for him.

By now, word had spread through Washington that the president had been shot, and a procession of government officials came running to the house, crowding into the room where Lincoln lay with a cluster of doctors at his side. Robert Lincoln, the president's oldest son, arrived with John Hay, barely hearing the words of the doctor who told them at the doorway to the room that it was no use. When he saw his father lying diagonally across the bed, his brain destroyed and his eye swollen and broken with blood, the usually calm and collected young man broke down in despair and disbelief. Finally, in shock himself, he went into the front parlor to try and comfort his mother. Mary had been sedated by one of the doctors and hardly knew he was there.

As Robert left the room, Senator Charles Sumner entered, his face twisted in anguish. The senator took Lincoln's hand and spoke to him but a doctor assured him that Lincoln was beyond hearing, that he was dead. "No, he isn't dead," Sumner protested in anger. "Look at his face, he is breathing." The other physicians assured him that Lincoln would never regain consciousness, and at that, Sumner clasped Lincoln's hand tightly, bowed his head close to the pillow and began to weep.

With the president's imminent death and the government at a standstill, Secretary of War Edwin Stanton took over. He set up a headquarters in the back parlor, and here a federal judge and two other men helped him to take testimony from the witnesses at the theater. All of them identified the assassin as John Wilkes Booth, the actor and Confederate sympathizer. At the same time, word came that another assassin had attempted but failed to murder Seward, and that Washington was being terrorized. At once, Stanton placed the city under martial law and ordered search parties to track down Booth and all other suspects.

As Stanton came and went, issuing orders, calling for Andrew Johnson and mobilizing troops and police officers, Mary lay on the sofa in the front parlor, going back and forth between eerie quiet and fits of weeping. She begged God to take her life too or trade her life for her husband's. Outside the windows of the Petersen house a crowd gathered in the foggy night, keeping a constant vigil and asking the officials who came and went if there was any word—or any hope.

It continued in this way throughout the night. The hours slowly passed and the doctors released half-hourly press bulletins about the president that went out over the telegraph lines. By dawn, the president's condition had worsened, and as the first gray light began to appear at the windows, a heavy rain began to fall, as if the heavens were weeping. Sumner was still holding Lincoln's hand when Mary came to see him one last time. She kissed his face and whispered to him: "Love, live but one moment to speak to me once." But then she looked at his shattered face and realized, perhaps for the first time, that he was beyond hope. She wailed as she was led away.

With the end close now, Lincoln's friends and colleagues gathered at his bedside. Edwin Stanton and Robert Lincoln came in from the front room, and Robert, giving away to his agony, put his head on Senator Sumner's shoulder. At that, many of the others present also began to cry. Finally, Lincoln took one great breath, his face relaxed and then he faded into oblivion.

The surgeon general carefully crossed the lifeless hands of Abraham Lincoln at twenty-two minutes after seven on the morning of April 15, 1865.

Edwin Stanton stood by the bedside of the slain president. He raised his head and with tears streaming down his face, uttered the most unforgettable words that a man not known for his poetic soul could ever manage: "Now, he belongs to the ages."

The Mystery of John Wilkes Booth

After shooting the president, John Wilkes Booth escaped from Washington on horseback across the Anacostia Bridge, passing a sentry who had not yet learned of the assassination. He made it to a farm in Virginia with the help of his fellow conspirators, only stopping to rest because of the leg that he broke when he jumped from the president's theater box.

Soon, the hunt for Lincoln's assassin was on, and by morning more than two thousand soldiers were looking for Booth. On April 26, a detachment of twenty-five men finally tracked down Booth and a comrade named David Herold at a tobacco farm near Port Royal, Virginia. The barn where they were hiding was surrounded and Herold decided to surrender. He was manacled and tied to a tree. Booth decided to die rather than be taken alive—or so the history books say.

In the darkness outside, a decision was made to try and smoke Booth out. The barn was set on fire and in a few moments, the interior was engulfed in flames. Booth came to the door and raised his weapon, apparently looking for a target among the soldiers outside. One of the soldiers, Sergeant Boston Corbett, saw Booth through the slats of the barn, and ignoring Edwin Stanton's specific orders to bring Booth back alive, shot him in the back of the head. Booth fell to the floor and the soldiers rushed to subdue him. He died two hours later, whispering instructions to tell his mother that he "died for his country and did what he thought best."

A search of the dead man's pockets turned up a few items, including a compass, a diary and photographs of several women, along with one portrait of Booth's fiancée, Lucy Hale.

Booth died on the porch of the farm house as light was beginning to show in the sky. The dead man was sewn into a burlap bag and was taken to Alexandria on a steamer. Booth's body was then placed on a carpenter's bench and identified from a crude tattoo of the actor's initials, by dental fillings and by a scar on the back of his neck. Others claimed that the body only resembled Booth, but that it actually wasn't him at all.

John Wilkes Booth in the burning barn. Harper's Weekly, *1865.*

Regardless, the corpse was taken to the Old Penitentiary in Washington, and using a gun case for a coffin, was buried under the floor of the old dining room. The door to the room was locked and the body stayed there for another four years. Finally, pleas from Edwin Booth convinced President Andrew Johnson to allow the body to be exhumed and buried in an unmarked grave in the family plot in Baltimore.

But was it really the body of John Wilkes Booth in the grave?

The man who shot Booth, Sergeant Boston Corbett, had been assigned to Lieutenant Edward Doherty and had been given the task of helping to track down the assassin. The soldiers found several witnesses who recognized Booth and eventually discovered sympathizer Willie Jett, who had arranged lodging for Booth at the tobacco farm where he was later discovered.

It was Corbett who fired the fatal bullet that killed Booth. It is at this point where many of the conspiracy theories begin. Among the theories is the idea that Corbett was under different orders than the other soldiers. Some believe he was actually told to silence Booth so that William Seward could not be implicated in the plot to kill Lincoln. It is unlikely that this was the case however, as Corbett is not believed to have had contact with Seward before leaving Washington. But the fact is, Corbett did act on orders to kill Booth, if not orders from government officials, then from a higher authority: he shot Booth on direct orders from God.

Corbett was a religious fanatic who believed that he was directed by voices from heaven. This is ironic considering that Booth also claimed to be acting on orders from God when he killed President Lincoln.

Corbett had been in the hat-making industry prior to the war and had been exposed to large quantities of mercury, which often caused insanity in this trade (thus, the expression "mad as a hatter"). Although he fought bravely in the Federal Army, his odd and erratic behavior often made his superiors wary about using him in some assignments. As a radical fundamentalist Christian, Corbett also reportedly castrated himself in 1858 after being solicited by a prostitute. Needless to say, this ended his temptation for fleshly sins. He also refused any alcohol and often condemned his fellow soldiers who drank.

Could Seward, or some other conspirator in the government, have used this unbalanced man as a pawn in the assassination plot? Perhaps, for he certainly would have followed any orders presented in a way that made him believe he was involved in some holy crusade.

After the war, Corbett moved to Kansas, where he became the security chief for the state legislature. He stayed in this position until one day when he pulled a gun on two boys who were mocking a minister's sermon. After that, he was committed to the Topeka Asylum for the Insane. He remained there until 1888, when Corbett escaped and seemingly vanished from the pages of history.

But the man who Corbett allegedly killed, while surely the murderer of Abraham Lincoln, didn't fade away quite so easily.

The newspapers quickly spread the word that President Lincoln's assassin, gunned down in a Virginia barn, was the actor John Wilkes Booth. There is no doubt in anyone's mind that the killer had been Booth, but the question remains as to whether or not Booth himself was ever brought to justice. That question still remains unanswered today.

Shortly after the assassin was gunned down, the word began to spread that it might not have been Booth in that barn after all. The government's handling of the body in question, and of the witnesses who were present, did not add much credence to the official version of the story. The Union soldiers had certainly killed a man. The War Department and the newspapers told a breathless nation that the man had been John Wilkes Booth—but was it really?

Autopsy of the man believed to be John Wilkes Booth. Harper's Weekly, *1866.*

From the day the body was brought back to Washington, there were already people on the streets denying the body was that of Booth. They believed the assassin had escaped and that the government was offering a secret substitution for the real killer.

The War Department took a firm position on the matter and would not argue it further. They maintained that the corpse was Booth's. In

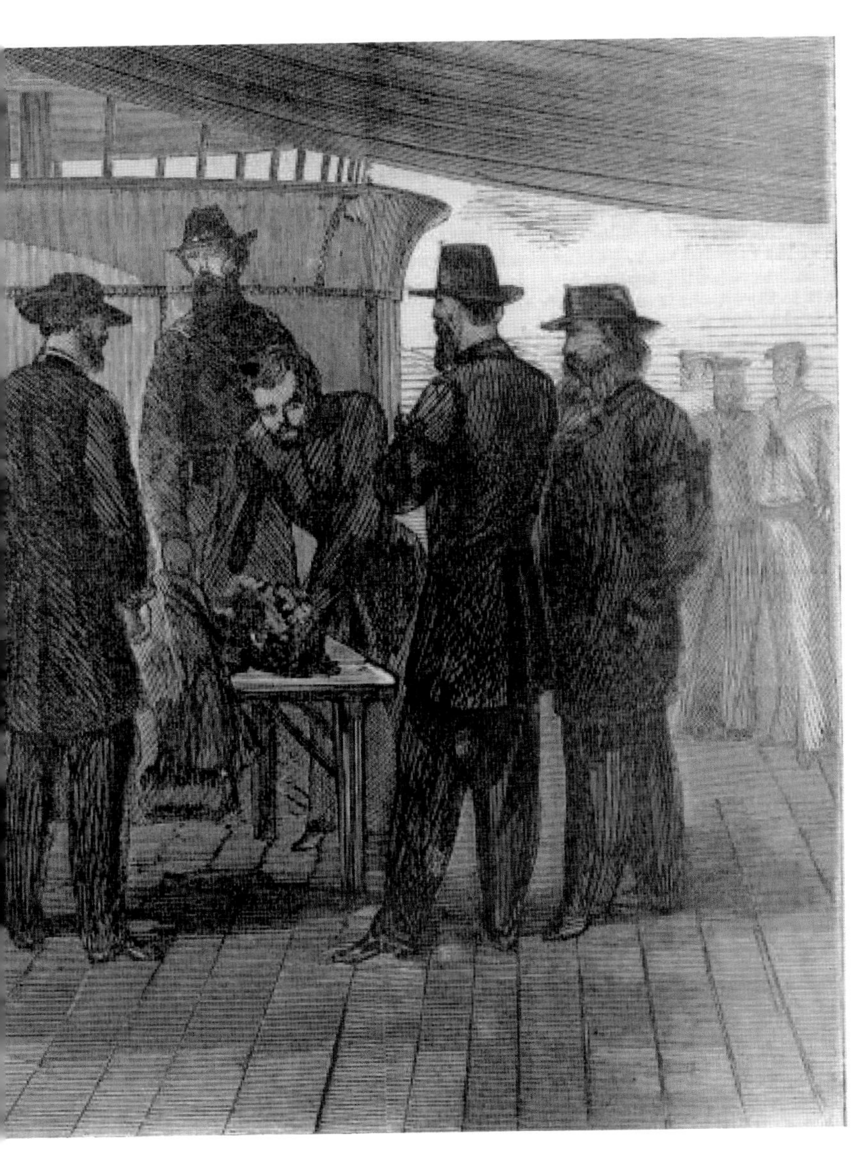

their possession were items that belonged to him and other evidence that proved they had the right man, including the left boot that Booth had abandoned to put his broken leg in splints, the revolver he had been carrying when killed and affidavits from the soldiers who brought the body back, claiming that the face of the corpse matched the photos of Booth they had been given. The investigators studied these, but they were never shown to the public. The government refused to even consider the idea that the body might not be that of Booth.

In the official silence from Washington, people began to see something dark and mysterious. They believed there was something strange about the attitude of the government toward Lincoln's murder and toward the killer. Perhaps those who believed in Booth's escape were right in their questioning. They were certainly correct in the knowledge that no one but government employees ever identified the body. It had been quickly hidden away with only certain people allowed to see it. There was not a single witness who was completely impartial, or free from suspicion, who could swear that he had looked at the face of the corpse and that the man had been John Wilkes Booth.

The mystery continued for many years. More than twenty men would later claim to be Booth with books, anecdotes and sworn testimony. The newspapers got hold of each story and fanned the flames of doubt. By June 1865 stories spread that witnesses had seen Booth on a steamer headed to Mexico, or to South America. It was said that several people saw him in the West and others recognized him in the Orient. In Ohio, a man claimed that Booth had stopped in his tavern on the way to Canada. In the Southwest, several people who claimed to know Booth said that he owed his escape to Union troopers, thanks to his membership in a fraternal order. They had spirited him away rather than see him hanged. It was no wonder that before long, dark haired, pallid men who walked with a limp began to be pointed out all across the country as John Wilkes Booth.

The story became so popular that in July 1867 Dr. John Frederick May, who had identified the body as Booth's, felt that it was now necessary to make an emphatic denial of his once positive identification. He now stated that he could have been wrong when he said the dead man had been John Wilkes Booth. It seems that two years before the assassination, May had removed a tumor from the back of Booth's neck. The surgery had left a jagged scar behind and this scar was how the doctor had identified the remains. He had been summoned to search for the mark of his scalpel on the corpse that he was supposed to identify.

May told of his experience:

> *The cover was removed from the body and to my great astonishment revealed a body in whose lineaments there was to me no resemblance to the man I had known in life. My surprise was so great that I at once said to General Barnes* [the U.S. Surgeon General that Stanton had sent to the inquest] *"There is no resemblance to Booth, nor can I believe it to be that of him." After looking at it a few moments I asked "Is there a scar upon the back of his neck?"*

He replied, "There is!"

I then said, "If that is the body of Booth, let me describe the scar before it is seen by man," and did so as to its position, its size and general appearance so accurately as to cause him to say, "You have described the scar as well as if you were looking at it." The body then being turned, the back of the neck was examined and my mark was unmistakably on it. And it being afterwards, at my request, placed in a sitting position and looking down upon it, I was finally enabled to imperfectly recognize the features of Booth. But never in a human being had a greater change taken place from the man in whom I had seen the vigor and health of life to that of the haggard corpse before me.[7]

This description by the surgeon failed to convince anyone that the body had really been Booth, especially as he continued, bringing to light a more damning bit of evidence. He explained in detail his examination of the corpse in question and its broken right leg. Now, the word of the government, and the witnesses at Ford Theater, said that Booth had broken his left leg when he jumped from the theater box. The fact that the doctor noted that the mysterious body had a broken right leg meant one of two things—either the body was not Booth's or Dr. May was too careless of an observer to be credited with any authority in the matter of an accurate identification.

Suspicion thrived across the country and by 1869, President Johnson decided to dispel of all the rumors and allow the assassin's brother to bury the disputed corpse in his family's cemetery plot. On February 15, 1869, government workers exhumed the body that had been buried beneath the floor of the old prison dining hall.

Many believed the mystery of the body would be settled once and for all by Edwin Booth, but he simply added to the confusion by bungling the whole thing. First he attempted to keep the exhumation a secret, and then he decided that he couldn't bear to look upon the face of his dead brother. He remained outside of the undertaker's room while friends went inside to examine the corpse. Not surprisingly, they decided the body belonged to John Wilkes Booth.

Needless to say, the public had a good mystery and they weren't about to let it go. A reporter for the *Baltimore Gazette* was soon claiming that he had been present at the exhumation and that the body had a broken right leg and no bullet holes in it. Modern historians believe this reporter had either a vivid imagination or lied about being at the exhumation at all. Still, in those days the story looked like new evidence that Booth was still alive.

The mystery continued into the twentieth century, and while Booth's skull was supposedly on display in a number of different traveling carnivals, there remained a question as to his eventual fate. Historians looked for answers in the early 1900s as many of the people involved in the case were still living. Statements were taken from surviving soldiers who aided in Booth's capture, and all information was thoroughly researched. They even checked out the claims of men still posing as Booth and found all of them to be transparently fraudulent.

Could Booth have survived the days after the assassination? The question nagged at historians, although logic would say that he had been killed. Still though, it is interesting that after all of the conflicting evidence there was not a single eyewitness sufficiently impartial to be above suspicion that had seen the corpse in 1865 and could say, with certainty, that it was John Wilkes Booth.

As mentioned, almost every single claim that Booth was alive was quickly exposed as a hoax. However, there were a few of them that weren't, and perhaps the most intriguing of these was the case of a man named David E. George, who died in Oklahoma in 1903.

Author W.C. Jameson explains that in order to understand the case of David George, the reader must also understand the history of Finis L. Bates, a young lawyer from Granbury, Texas. Bates was struggling to earn a living in the early 1870s, and must have been happy when a man who called himself John St. Helen strolled into his office one day and asked the attorney to defend him against a charge of operating a saloon without a license in the nearby town of Glen Rose. He admitted that he was guilty of the charge but that he did not want to appear in federal court over it. John St. Helen was not his real name, he confessed, and he feared that his identity might be exposed in court.

Bates soon became the man's lawyer and got to know him quite well. He stated that St. Helen seemed to have more money than his status should have allowed and that he had an intimate knowledge of the theater and of the works of Shakespeare, most of which he could recite from memory.

Then, late one night in 1877, Bates was summoned to the sickbed of his client. He was seriously ill and he told Bates that he did not expect to live much longer. He told Bates to reach under his pillow and the attorney took out an old tintype that showed a much younger St. Helen. The sick man told the attorney that if he died, he was to send the photograph to an

Edwin Booth in Baltimore with a note that said the subject of the tintype had passed away. In between coughing fits, St. Helen explained to the stunned attorney that his name was actually John Wilkes Booth and that he had assassinated former President Abraham Lincoln.

Bates was shocked and dismayed at the revelation, but he knew that he could not betray his client's confidence. He replied that he would send the photograph if needed and he sat next to St. Helen's bed throughout the rest of the night. No one knows what thoughts must have been churning in the young man's mind.

However, St. Helen did not die. He remained sick for several weeks but eventually began to recover. Once he was mobile again, he met with Bates and again confessed to being John Wilkes Booth. He begged for the attorney to keep the secret, and Bates had no ethical choice but to agree. He did demand some answers, though, knowing full well that John Wilkes Booth was reportedly dead.

Booth explained that Andrew Johnson, the vice president, was the principle conspirator behind the assassination. (Interestingly, many theorists agree with this and a number of scenarios exist to explain Johnson's motives.) St. Helen said that he had met with Johnson just hours before Lincoln was killed and Johnson told him that with General Grant away from Washington, Booth would have an easy escape route into Maryland. St. Helen then went on to provide details of the assassination plot, the actual event, his escape from Ford's Theater and flight into the countryside. His descriptions were detailed and to Bates, who initially believed none of the far-fetched story, seemed to have intricacies that only someone intimately involved with the assassination plot would have known. Most of all, they were different enough from the already published accounts of the events that Bates began to give some credibility to St. Helen's version of the story.

St. Helen told the attorney that he had escaped into Kentucky in late April and eventually made his way west of the Mississippi and into the Indian Territory. After spending some time there, he disguised himself as a priest and entered Mexico. In 1867, he traveled to California and met with his mother and older brother Junius in San Francisco. Later, he drifted to New Orleans, where he taught school, and then moved to Texas. Here, he assumed the name John St. Helen and opened a tavern.

He was, he insisted, the assassin known as John Wilkes Booth, and Bates kept the story to himself. Eventually, the two men parted ways. Several months after St. Helen's confession, Bates moved to Memphis and established what became a very successful law practice. As the years passed, he developed a deep interest in Abraham Lincoln, especially in the events surrounding his death. In his spare time, he read everything that he could get his hands on about Lincoln and Booth—and the more he studied, the more convinced he became that his old client was indeed telling the truth.

John St. Helen, he realized, really had been John Wilkes Booth!

The story of John Wilkes Booth and Finis Bates took another turn in January 1903. On the 13th of that month, the corpse of a man named David E. George arrived at the undertaking parlor of W.B. Penniman in Enid, Oklahoma. George, who had been working in Enid as a handyman and house painter, had apparently committed suicide by ingesting a large dose of strychnine. He was already known as a heavy drinker and was thought to have been depressed of late.

As Penniman's assistant, W.H. Ryan, was embalming George's body, the Reverend E.C. Harper stopped in to the funeral parlor. Harper went into the embalming room, and surprised to see the body there, asked Ryan if he knew who the man was. Rev. Harper explained that the dead man was none other than John Wilkes Booth, and that he had confessed his identity to the minister's wife in 1900. Mrs. Harper was summoned and she identified the corpse of David E. George as the man who had told her that he was Booth. She later wrote out and signed a statement, swearing that the confession had taken place.

Over the course of the next few days, a number of newspapers carried the story that a man believed to be Booth had died in Oklahoma. One of the newspaper stories caught the attention of Finis Bates in Memphis and he wondered if the late David E. George might be the man that he had once known as John St. Helen. Curious, he decided to go to Enid and see.

Bates arrived in Oklahoma on January 23, and the next morning, went to the undertaker's establishment to compare the face of the dead man with the tintype photograph that he still possessed. He placed it next to the face of the corpse and compared them. It was, Bates stated without a doubt, the same man!

The body remained on display at Penniman's parlor, and after it went unclaimed for some time, it was eventually moved into a back room and stored for several years. Eventually, Bates purchased the body and he kept it for many years. In October 1931 the mummy was examined by a group of seven doctors at Chicago's Northwestern University. It was studied, x-rayed and dissected, and the team did find evidence of a broken leg, although the

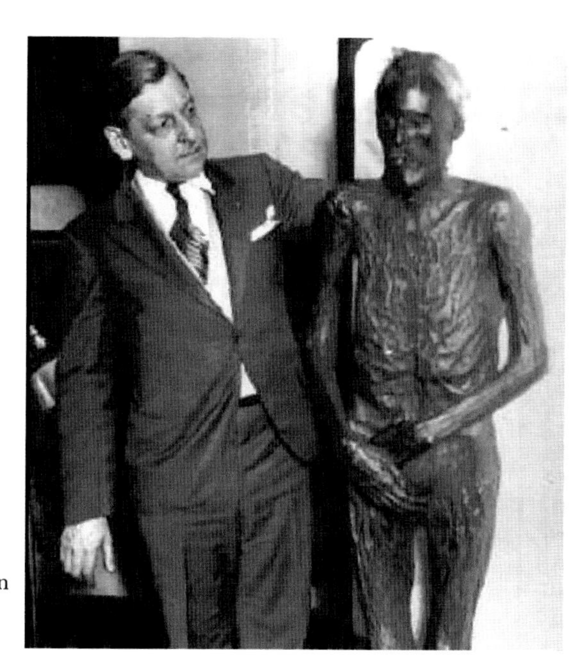

A photo of the mummy of David E. George, exhibited in sideshows for years as John Wilkes Booth. *E.H. Swaim Collection.*

report did not state whether it was the right or the left. The most compelling discovery was that of a ring that had somehow become embedded in the flesh of the stomach cavity. Digestive juices had damaged it over time, but the researchers present believed that the initials "JWB" could be discerned on the surface of it. Dr. Otto L. Schmidt, who was present and who was the president of the Chicago Historical Society at that time, subsequently wrote: "I can say safely that we believe Booth's body is here in my office."

The fate of this intriguing mummy remains a mystery. At one point, Bates tried to sell it to the *Dearborn Independent* for $10,000, and at another time offered it to Henry Ford for $100,000, but it was declined both times. During the 1920s and 1930s, Bates leased the mummy to a carnival promoter who charged twenty-five cents to view "The Assassin of President Abraham Lincoln." The mummy was still being displayed into the 1940s, but after the promoter went bankrupt and moved to Idaho, he placed the mummy in a chair on his front porch and charged visitors a dime to look at it. Eventually, the mummy disappeared and to this day, no one knows what became of it. It is rumored to be in a private collection somewhere but no one knows for sure.

The final resting place of the mummy is just as mysterious as the questions that linger about John Wilkes Booth. Were Booth and St. Helen/George the same man? Although many feel that Bates tried too hard to make Booth and George appear to be the same, it can't be ignored that they possessed many of the same characteristics, including heavy drinking, an intimate knowledge of Shakespeare, a penchant for the theater, the same style of dress and the fact that the men were well-educated. In addition, studies of physical characteristics between George and Booth showed many striking similarities, including the shape of their heads, jaw lines and the bridges of both men's noses. And while this doesn't really prove anything, it does make some researchers wonder.

There are many problems with the theory, as well. Skeptics state that the color of George's eyes were enough to debunk his claims. His eyes, according to the undertaker, were bluish gray, while government documents say Booth's were black. On the other hand, Asia Booth, the actor's sister, wrote that they were hazel. They also say that Bates wrote that George had a broken right leg, not the left leg that Booth broke jumping from the theater box. Of course, the government's own records stated that the body that was dug up from beneath the floor of the Old Penitentiary had a broken right leg. So, which records were accurate and which were not?

Bates showed photographs of St. Helen and George to a number of people who had known Booth, including those who had seen him perform many times. All of them stated that the man in both photos was John Wilkes Booth.

Another mysterious piece of evidence involved the signet ring worn by Booth. The actor was seldom seen without the ring, which was inscribed with his initials, and he was photographed wearing it many times. The ring was not on the finger of the man who was killed in Virginia. David E. George wore a similar ring, many recalled. Some weeks before his death, George told one of his neighbors that he was being followed. One afternoon, when he saw two sheriff deputies coming his way, George was so afraid that he would be identified that he removed the ring from his finger and swallowed it. This strange anecdote would provide startling evidence to researchers in 1931 that the body they were examining (with a ring inside of the stomach cavity) was that of John Wilkes Booth.

But was it? Who knows? The evidence for the man from Oklahoma being John Wilkes Booth is certainly plausible, but unfortunately so much time has passed, and so much evidence has been lost, that the answers will likely never be known.

The tragic events of that Good Friday evening in 1865 sparked another chain of events involving people closely embroiled in the assassination. When Booth jumped from the theater box that night, he left behind not only a dead president, but several shattered lives as well—all of them destined to meet tragic ends.

The Curse of Mary Lincoln

Mary Lincoln. *Library of Congress.*

Mary Lincoln, whose mental state had already been declining since the death of her son, Willie, in 1862, never recovered from the loss of her husband. She struggled with family problems and more heartbreak, and eventually was committed to a mental institution for a time.

Her curse would be that she managed to live seventeen years after the death of her husband. For months after his murder, Mary spoke of nothing but the assassination until her friends began to drift away, their sympathy at a breaking point. She began to accuse her husband's friends and his cabinet members of complicity in the murder, from his bodyguards to Andrew Johnson.

Mary lay in her bed for forty days after the assassination and in the years that followed, she deteriorated mentally and physically into a bitter old woman who wore nothing but black mourning clothing for the rest of her life.

Mary had a great fear of poverty. She often begged her friends to help her with money. Unlike the widows of generals and governors, for whom money was easily raised, Mary's handful of supporters found it impossible to raise funds on her behalf because she was just too unpopular. In fact, she was despised all across America. Newspapers wrote unflattering stories about her and she was ridiculed by members of Washington society.

In 1868, she abandoned America and took her youngest son, Tad, to live in Germany. They lived there in hiding for three years before coming home. A government pension awaited her, as did an inheritance from Lincoln's estate, so she was finally a wealthy woman. The ocean crossing had dire consequences for Tad, however. He developed tuberculosis, and although he lingered for six weeks, he eventually passed away.

In the spring of 1875, Robert Lincoln decided to have his mother institutionalized. He was concerned not only for her sanity, but for her estate as well, which he claimed some of her unscrupulous "friends" had designs on. By this time, Robert was wealthy in his own right and had no plans for his mother's money, which Mary refused to understand. He did, however, hire detectives to follow his mother and gather information about her drug use, which included opium, and he paid doctors to testify about her sanity in court.

Mary was sent to a mental hospital but was later released. She severed all ties with Robert, calling him a "wicked monster." She would hate him for the rest of her days, and before she died, she wrote him letters that cursed him and claimed that his father had never really loved him.

Mary went into exile again and moved into a small hotel in France. Her eyes were weakened and her body was wracked with pain from severe arthritis. She refused to travel until several bad falls left her nearly unable to walk. Her sister pleaded with her to come home and finally she returned to Springfield, Illinois, moving into the same house where she and Lincoln had been married years before.

Mary lived the last years of her life in a single room, wearing a money belt to protect her fortune. She kept all of the shades in her room drawn and spent her days packing and unpacking her sixty-four crates of clothing. She died on July 12, 1882—a faded shell of the exuberant young socialite that she had once been.

THE "LINCOLN CURSE"

The president's oldest son, Robert, was also no stranger to death and foreboding. He was the only Lincoln son to survive into adulthood, and by the time he died in 1926, he was a very haunted man. He believed wholeheartedly that a curse hung over his life.

Robert Lincoln. *Library of Congress.*

His strange belief began in 1865 when he was with his father at the time of his death. Needless to say, it was an event that he would never forget.

Sixteen years later, in 1881, Robert was connected to another American president whose life was ended by an assassin. President James Garfield, who had only been in office about four months, was walking through the railroad station in Washington when suddenly a crazed killer named Charles Guiteau appeared from nowhere and gunned him down.

Robert Lincoln was Garfield's secretary of war, and just a few days before Garfield was shot, the president asked to meet with Robert. He asked Robert several questions about his father's assassination and Robert tried to recall as much about the event as he could. The two men spoke for about an hour. Just two days later, Garfield was shot.

In 1901, President William McKinley invited Robert Lincoln to tour the Pan-American Exposition with him in Buffalo, New York. While the two men were together, an anarchist named Leon Czolgosg managed to approach them with a pistol. In seconds, President McKinley was dead.

For the third time, Robert had been present at the death of an American president.

Not surprisingly, he became convinced that he was "cursed" and that somehow he had contributed to the deaths of these men, including the death of his father. From that time on, he refused to ever meet, or even be near, another American president. Although invitations arrived from the White House, and from other Washington social gatherings, he declined them all.

Was there truly a curse over Robert Lincoln's head? He certainly believed there was.

THE TRAGEDY OF CLARA HARRIS & MAJOR HENRY RATHBONE

Major Henry Rathbone, who was stabbed by Booth, recovered physically from the attack but would forever be haunted by the terrible night of the assassination.

Following the assassination, the traumatized Clara returned home for a time and stayed with her parents at their house in Loudonville, New York, just north of Albany. Clara brought with her the gown that she had been wearing on the night Lincoln was killed, the fine fabric streaked and stained with the president's blood. In order to preserve the dress for all eternity, she is said to have placed it in a closet and then ordered the chamber to be walled shut.

After Clara returned to Washington, she and Major Rathbone were soon married. Rathbone retired from military service and the couple moved to Germany, but the marriage was anything but blissful. Clara found that her husband was prone to bouts of depression and moodiness, none of which he had been inclined toward before the night in Ford's Theater. Then one morning, on Christmas Day 1883, he went over the edge and killed Clara in a fit of insanity. Their children were spared, thanks to the bravery of their nanny, and Rathbone failed in his attempt to take his own life. He managed to stab himself four times, but lived long enough to die in a German mental institution in 1911.

THE MYSTERY OF MARY SURRATT

Mary Surratt's trial was possibly one of the great travesties of American justice. She had been the proprietor of a Washington boardinghouse where John Wilkes Booth had stayed while plotting the kidnapping, and

The execution of the Lincoln assassination conspirators. Mary Surratt can be seen on the far left. *Library of Congress.*

then murder, of Abraham Lincoln. At midnight, on the same night that Lincoln had been shot, Mary was rousted from her bed by police officers and federal troops. She was accused of being a conspirator in Lincoln's death and was taken to the prison at the Old Brick Capitol. From that point on, Mary never stopped insisting that she was innocent and that she barely knew Booth, but no one listened.

The testimonies of two people were instrumental in Mary's conviction. One of them was a notorious drunk and the other was a known liar, a former policeman to whom Mary had leased her tavern in Maryland. At the trial's conclusion, she and three other defendants were found guilty and sentenced to death by hanging. Mary Surratt was the last of the four to die on July 7, 1865.

It is true that Mary may not have been as blameless as she claimed to be. Besides Booth, the other residents of the boardinghouse included her son, John, who was a Confederate courier, and several Southern sympathizers. It is possible that she knew more than she claimed to, but it is still doubtful that she was in any way involved in the murder plot. To say that the evidence against her was circumstantial is a gross understatement, and in light of that and other factors, the punishment certainly was much harsher than what was believed to be her crime.

Even though Mary Surratt was sentenced to die, the board that convicted her sent a petition to President Andrew Johnson to ask that her sentence be commuted to life in prison. Whether this is because she was a woman or because they had doubts about her guilt is unknown. The commander of the federal troops in Washington was so sure that a last minute reprieve would arrive that he stationed messengers on horseback along the shortest route from the White House to the Washington Arsenal Prison, where the execution was to take place.

Until the time the hood was placed over her head, officials in charge of the execution were sure that Mary would be spared. While four of the defendants died that day, three others received long prison sentences, including the famous Dr. Samuel Mudd. John Surratt, who had fled to Canada, was later returned for trial, but was acquitted. What actually forced the hand of the judge to sentence Mary to death, and what stopped President Johnson from issuing the reprieve, is unknown because many historians today believe that Mary Surratt was innocent.

Mary Surratt's life was merely another that was ruined in the wake of the death of the president.

HIS NAME WAS MUDD

On April 15, 1865, a loud pounding at the front door awakened Dr. Samuel Mudd from a deep sleep. He had been resting in one of the upstairs bedrooms of his farmhouse in Charles County, Maryland,

Dr. Samuel Mudd. *National Archives.*

about three miles from Beantown. No stranger to urgent calls in the middle of the night, the doctor hurried downstairs and opened his home to two men. One of them was badly in need of medical attention so Dr. Mudd decided to allow them in.

Little did he know that this decision would not only entangle him in the Lincoln assassination conspiracy, but it would also make him a part of one of the greatest mysteries of the time. Was Dr. Mudd simply an innocent doctor assisting an injured man or did he aid John Wilkes Booth in his escape from Washington?

Dr. Mudd would later admit to the fact that he had met one of the late night callers, John Wilkes Booth, on an earlier occasion, but he claimed that on that April morning he did not recognize him or his companion, David Herold. The two men were wearing makeshift disguises at the time and it is possible that Mudd truly did not recognize Booth. He would always maintain that he was simply administering to an injured man, and that he was more interested in Booth's broken leg than in his identity.

Dr. Mudd proceeded to set Booth's leg and the two men were given food and rest until the afternoon of the same day. They left the house toward evening and headed toward Zekiah Swamp, reportedly never revealing their identities or how Booth came to be injured.

Several days later, Dr. Mudd was arrested for his alleged role in the Lincoln assassination. He was tried and convicted by the military court and was sentenced to life in prison at Fort Jefferson, located on Dry Tortugas Island in Florida. He remained there for four years, until he was pardoned by President Andrew Johnson. The pardon was not because of new evidence that proved Mudd to be innocent but because of a request that had been signed by the warden, the officials and all of the inmates at the Florida prison. They believed they owed the doctor their lives after his aid during a Yellow Fever epidemic that swept through the prison.

There is still disagreement today over Mudd's role in the assassination. It is known that he was a Southern sympathizer, as were most of the residents of southern Maryland, but it is also known that federal officials "rushed to judgment" in the aftermath of Lincoln's death. They were anxious to catch anyone who might have been in any way involved in the murder, and it's possible that potentially innocent people like Dr. Mudd, and perhaps Mary Surratt, may have been caught in the frenzy.

So, was Dr. Mudd guilty of conspiring in Lincoln's assassination? That question remains a mystery and one that continues to be debated to this day.

4.

The Forgotten Assassination

The Death of President James Garfield

Abraham Lincoln was the first American president to be slain while in office, but he would not be the last. Many readers can still remember today where they were and what they were doing when word reached them of the assassination of John F. Kennedy. In 1900, when President William McKinley was killed, he became a fallen martyr to the nation and scores of commemorative books were printed in his honor. But there was one murdered president that few seem to recall today, and if asked, most would not even recall his name.

James Garfield never set out to become president. The former Civil War general and college president never had any loftier goals in mind than representing Ohio in Congress. After sixteen years in the House, he was elected to the Senate in 1880. Before he was able to take office, though, events at the Republican National Convention conspired to forever change his life. Garfield was heading the Ohio delegation at the convention and he found the party was hopelessly divided into two factions. One group of Republicans, the "Stalwart" faction, supported former U.S. President Ulysses S. Grant, who was seeking a third term, and the more progressive "Half-Breeds" wanted Senator James G. Blaine of Maine as the nominee. Somehow, out of all of this confusion, Garfield's name was put into the mix and the more that people talked about it, the more promising a candidate he became.

When Garfield was warned by a friend that there had been talk of nominating him as the Republican candidate, Garfield was perturbed: "My God! I know it. I know it! They will ruin me. I am here as a friend

President James Garfield. *Library of Congress.*

of Sherman [John Sherman was another hopeful Republican candidate] and what will he and the world think of me if I am put in nomination? I won't permit it!"

Garfield was convinced to accept the nomination for the good of the country, and when the election was over, he had managed to defeat his Democratic opponent, General Winfield Scott Hancock. The idea of being president never ceased to trouble him. He wrote: "I am bidding goodbye to private life and to a long period of happy years which I feel will terminate in 1880."

In those days, incoming presidents faced the overwhelming task of filling thousands of government jobs left open when workers from the previous administration were automatically fired when the former president left office. Most of Garfield's time as president was taken up by this task, which he despised. He often complained: "My services ought to be worth more to the government than to be thus spent."

Everywhere that he went, hordes of office seekers harassed him. Thousands filed into the White House, looking for jobs. In those days, security at the White House was almost nonexistent, even though Abraham Lincoln had been murdered less than two decades before. Ironically, on the very day that he was killed, Lincoln had signed an order that created the U.S. Secret Service. Unfortunately, it would be many years before the department was assigned to the task of protecting the president. At that time, their sole mission was to track down and arrest counterfeiters.

At the time Garfield took office, almost anyone could walk into the White House and ask to see the president. Job seekers managed to get into almost every corner of the mansion and clogged Pennsylvania Avenue every morning. Garfield groaned: "These people would take my very brain, flesh and blood if they could."

One of the most persistent hopefuls was a man named Charles Julius Guiteau, a mentally unbalanced drifter who had failed at everything he had ever tried—except, as it turned out, assassinating the president of the United States.

Charles Julius Guiteau was born in Freeport, Illinois, in September 1841. He was raised in a fervently religious family where beatings were common. Charles was always considered to be a "little different" by neighbors and members of the community. He was unruly and plagued by a speech impediment for which his father often whipped him. Perhaps because of this, he developed precocious skills at reading and writing.

In 1860, Guiteau hooked up with a utopian religious community in New York but came to believe that he had been divinely chosen to lead the cult—and to bed as many of the female members as possible. Such claims did not sit well with the community leaders, or with the ladies, and he was sent packing in April 1865.

He headed to New York City with plans to start a religious newspaper and to spearhead a national spiritual awakening. His plans failed when banks refused to loan him start-up money, so he decided to try his hand at evangelism instead. Adorned with sandwich board signs, Guiteau walked the streets, inviting everyone to listen to his sermons on the physical existence of hell and the Second Coming of Christ. His scheme fizzled, though, when audiences either laughed or became angry at his incoherent sermons. He was soon driven out of town, leaving unpaid bills and a collection of arrests behind.

Describing himself as a "lawyer, theologian and politician," Guiteau next sought the Republican presidential nomination in 1880. Ignored, ridiculed and often chased away from party headquarters, Guiteau moved to Washington in March 1881. Somehow, he became convinced that he was responsible for Garfield's election and decided that the office of consul general in Paris was a fitting reward for his services. He began coming to the White House each day, badgering the president's staff and even Garfield himself. One day, he took a copy of a disjointed speech that he had written for Garfield's campaign, scrawled the words "Paris Consulship" and shoved it into the bewildered president's hands. When he received no response, Guiteau returned to the White House again and again. The nervous little man with the unkempt beard and haunted stare spent weeks frightening staff members and handing letters to busy politicians.

A frequent target of Guiteau's harassment was Secretary of State James G. Blaine. He constantly bothered Blaine for his high level appointment, and eventually Blaine had the strange little man barred from the premises.

The offended Guiteau fired off a letter to President Garfield, demanding that he fire Blaine at once. He wrote: "Otherwise, you and the Republican Party will come to grief… Mr. Blaine is a wicked man, an evil genius… and you will have no peace till you get rid of him."

When Garfield ignored Guiteau's letter, an idea began to form in the disturbed man's mind. He would kill the president, after which he would be proclaimed a hero and savior of the Republican Party, then would be elected by a grateful nation to succeed the deposed "traitor."

On June 8, 1881, Guiteau borrowed the money to purchase a revolver, and then after practicing with it for several days, he began stalking the president, waiting for the perfect opportunity to kill him.

His chance came less than a month later, on Saturday, July 2, when the president arrived at the Baltimore & Potomac Railroad Station, which was then on the Washington Mall. Earlier that morning, Guiteau had placed his gun in his coat and had made his way through the crowds to await the president's arrival. Before he had left his home, he had written a note to the press: "I had no ill will toward the president. His death was a political necessity."

President Garfield was deep in conversation with Secretary of State Blaine and was oblivious to the assassin's approach. Guiteau ran up behind him, and from less than a yard away, fired his pistol into Garfield's back. The stunned president stumbled forward and fell to the ground. Guiteau took two steps forward and shot him again. As he raised his pistol, he shouted: "I am a Stalwart and [Vice President Chester] Arthur is president now!"

A police officer who was standing nearby tackled Guiteau, who tried in vain to escape. Onlookers, finally realizing what had just occurred, demanded that the little man be hanged on the spot. It was all that the policeman could do keep them away from him.

Meanwhile, President Garfield was sprawled on the station floor. One of the bullets had grazed his arm, but the other was deep in his body. At the time, sterilization of wounds and instruments was still not commonplace, and a physician, seeking the bullet, probed at the wound with unwashed

The assassination of James Garfield. Harper's Weekly, *1881.*

fingers. Believing that the president was bleeding internally, the doctor reassured him that the wound was not serious. But Garfield, rapidly losing consciousness, thought otherwise. He smiled weakly before managing a few words: "Thank you, doctor, but I am a dead man."

The president was taken to the White House, where he lingered near death with the bullet still inside of him. Medical advice poured in from all over the country. One of those who inquired on the president's life was Alexander Graham Bell, the famous inventor. Using one of his telephone receivers, Bell rigged up a crude metal detector device that would create a disturbance in an electrical circuit when it came near the missing bullet. This disturbance would cause a hum in the telephone receiver. X-ray machines would not be invented for another decade, far too late for the ailing president, and so, thanks to Bell's worldwide fame, Garfield's doctors agreed to give the invention a try.

Bell came to the White House and hooked up the machine. With the president propped up in bed, he listened closely to the receiver as an assistant slowly moved electrical coils across Garfield's abdomen and back. He finally heard a hum! The bullet was near a black-and-blue spot where the doctors had assumed it had ended up. The problem was that it was much deeper than they first surmised. Because of this, they felt that major surgery would be too hazardous to attempt.

Not long after this, Garfield rallied enough to be taken to a seaside cottage in Elberon, New Jersey, in hopes that he might recover. He didn't. In fact, a few days later an infection set in and Garfield's temperature began to climb. The doctors opened the original incision that was made by the physician and his dirty fingers and enlarged it outward and downward, as Bell had suggested. The bullet was never removed. James Garfield died on September 19, 1881, well over two months after being shot.

Many medical historians believe that Garfield probably would not have died if the bullet had been left alone. What killed him, they believe, was not the bullet, which became wrapped in a protective cyst, but infections caused by instruments and hands that were not sterile. They caused infections against which Garfield had no resistance, since he had been lying in bed for two months.

An autopsy that followed found the missing bullet—a full ten inches deeper than the doctors and Bell believed it to be. What was the hum that was heard by Bell, his assistant, the doctors and Mrs. Garfield? Was the machine actually working? It might have been, but some believe that it was picking up the metal of the bedspring under the president's body rather than the bullet. No one knows for sure, but Bell's invention did not turn out to be a total loss. Later, in a more elaborate form, it was used by the military for the detection of land mines.

As Americans mourned a president who never really had a chance to govern the country, his assassin was put on trial in Washington. The courtroom had a circus-like atmosphere. Guiteau, who entered a "not guilty by reason of temporary insanity" plea, maintained that his madness was brought upon him by "divine power." At the trial, attorney George Scoville—Guiteau's brother-in-law—argued that his client truly was insane. Guiteau's mother as well as several aunts, cousins and uncles all suffered from mental problems. His sister, Scoville's wife, was institutionalized in October 1882. Whether or not Guiteau helped or hindered his defense is debatable. He constantly interrupted the proceedings with shouts and weird ranting. He called the prosecutor a "low-livered whelp" and all of the witnesses against him "dirty liars." At the conclusion of the lengthy trial, he insisted on making his own summation before the jury. He yelled at them: "God told me to kill. Let your verdict be that it was the Deity's act, not mine."

Charles Guiteau. Harper's Weekly, *1881.*

If Guiteau really was insane (and it certainly seems likely that he was), the jury was not interested in letting him off for his crimes. He was convicted and sentenced to death by hanging at the Washington Asylum and Jail. He went to the gallows on June 30, 1882. He was happy to go because he had finally achieved what he had wanted all along—to be the center of the nation's attention.

5.

Presidential Scandals

Washington is, without a doubt, the most scandal-ridden, gossip-filled city in the United States. It is also a city that gives birth to legend and rumor, where a single whispered allegation can grow to mammoth proportions within hours. And where a lone truth or an unsubstantiated lie can destroy careers and wreck lives.

Such has been the case with not only the ordinary people of Washington but also with the politicians, military men and even those who hold the greatest power in the country—the presidents of the United States. How many of them have been falsely accused of scandal and how many have been guilty of contributing their share to the stuff of legend that still swirls about the White House today?

Read on and I think you just might be surprised!

The Mysterious Death of Warren G. Harding

Warren G. Harding, our twenty-ninth American president, held office from 1921 to 1923 and has been regarded by many historians as the worst president ever to serve. Even Harding himself seemed to agree. He was often quoted as saying: "I am not fit for this office and never should have been here." His administration was considered to be one of the most corrupt in American history, and personal scandals often overshadowed the better aspects of his presidency (such as the peace treaties that he signed leading to the end of World War I and to naval disarmament). But

Warren G. Harding. *National Archives.*

perhaps the greatest of the scandals concerning President Harding was the questions that surrounded his death.

It has become another of Washington's weird mysteries and it will likely never be solved. Many claim that the cause of his death, which occurred on August 2, 1923, has never been truly established. The White House initially said that it was from food poisoning; a physician stated that it was due to a cerebral hemorrhage; and still another claimed that it was a heart attack. Which was it? We may never know.

Warren G. Harding was born in Ohio on November 2, 1865, and got his start in business there after his father purchased a local weekly newspaper. After attending Ohio Central College, he moved to Marion and raised the three hundred dollars needed to purchase a failing newspaper called the *Daily Star*. It was the only daily newspaper in the city but was in bad need of help. He quickly converted the editorial platform to support the Republicans and began enjoying a decent amount of success. However, his views clashed with those who controlled most of Marion's local politics and he soon attracted unwanted attention. When Harding moved to try and unseat the *Marion Independent* as the official paper of daily record, his actions angered Amos Hall Kling, a wealthy real estate speculator.

Harding eventually won the battle and his newspaper became one of the largest in the county, but the conflict took a toll on his health. In 1889, he began suffering from exhaustion and nervous fatigue and traveled to Battle Creek, Michigan, where he spent several weeks at a sanatorium to regain his strength. He later returned to Marion and continued running the paper.

On July 8, 1891, Harding married Florence Mable Kling DeWolfe, a shrill, dowdy divorcée. The tall and mannish woman had pursued Harding without mercy until he reluctantly surrendered and proposed to her. Many claim that it was Florence's constant harassment of Harding that actually led him to spend his weeks at the Battle Creek Sanatorium enduring J.P. Kellogg's crackpot "cures" and enema therapies. Florence's father was Amos Hall Kling, Harding's enemy. When he heard that his only daughter intended to marry Harding, Kling disowned her and even prevented his wife from attending the wedding. He continued to oppose the marriage for the next eight years and did not speak to his daughter or son-in-law during that time.

It was a miserable marriage and Harding was said to have submitted weakly to Florence's domination. He gave her the nickname of "The Duchess," but it was, without question, her business sense that made Harding a financial and political success. She ran the newspaper with crisp efficiency and plotted his unlikely political ascent.

Harding became active in politics in the late 1890s, serving in the state Senate for four years before winning election as the lieutenant governor of Ohio. His time in office was undistinguished, and at the conclusion of his term in 1905, he returned to public life.

Florence would not let him stay there for long. In 1912, she wrangled him the chance to give the nominating speech for incumbent President William Taft at the Republican Convention. In 1914, with the help of political boss Harry Daughtery, Harding was elected to the U.S. Senate.

Florence Harding, the intimidating "Duchess." *Library of Congress.*

During his years in the Senate, Harding missed over two-thirds of all roll calls and votes, compiling one of the worst attendance records in history. He introduced only one hundred and thirty-four bills, none of them significant. In spite of this, Harding was always seen as affable and was well-liked by his colleagues. He was a loyal party man and worked to keep harmony. This turned out to be a great help to him in 1920, when a deadlocked Republican convention turned to Harding as a compromise candidate.

Harding's time in the Senate was also marked with the first scandal to influence his career. A press secretary named Erin Gaertner accused him of having sex with her. The story made the newspapers for a bit, but eventually went away.

Harding's presidential efforts were referred to as his "front porch campaign" and the campaign was carried out during the late summer and fall of 1920. It managed to capture the imagination of the public, thanks to the fact that it was heavily covered by the press, received widespread newsreel coverage and was also the first campaign to really use the influence of Hollywood and Broadway stars. Celebrities like Al Jolson, Lillian Russell, Douglas Fairbanks and Mary Pickford took part in photo opportunities with Harding, and business legends like Thomas Edison, Henry Ford and Harvey Firestone also lent their names to the campaign.

All of this hoopla owed a great deal to Florence Harding, who played perhaps a more active role than any previous candidate's wife in a presidential campaign. She cultivated the relationship between the campaign and the press, posed for pictures, answered questions and made sure of a steady delivery of food to the press office, a bungalow that she had arranged to have built at the rear of the Harding property in Marion. Florence even went so far as to coach her husband on the proper way to wave for the newsreel cameras.

The campaign also took advantage of Harding's popularity with women. Considered handsome, Harding photographed well, especially in comparison to his opponent, Ohio governor James Cox. But it was Harding's support for women's suffrage in the Senate that made him most popular with the ladies. The ratification of the nineteenth Amendment, giving women the vote, in August 1920 brought huge crowds of women to Marion to see the candidate.

At least once, the campaign took a nasty turn. Rumors were spread that Harding's great-great-grandfather was a black man from the West Indies and that other blacks might be found in his family tree. This was a volatile charge at a time when the Ku Klux Klan was seeing a resurgence in popularity, but Harding's campaign manager dismissed the story: "No family in the state has a clearer, more honorable record than the Hardings, a blue-eyed stock from New England and Pennsylvania, the finest pioneer blood." The story was likely just a local rumor but many believe that it got out of hand because of an alleged response that Harding gave to a reporter who asked him about it: "How do I know Jim? One of my ancestors may have jumped the fence." Florence Harding was likely not very happy with his joking response.

In the end, rumors had little effect on the vote. With women finally able to cast a ballot in the election, Harding received 61 percent of the national vote and 404 electoral votes, which was an unprecedented margin of victory.

Harding made a number of excellent appointments in his new administration. Charles Hughes was named as secretary of state, Andrew Mellon became secretary of the treasury, Herbert Hoover became secretary of commerce, Charles Dawes became director of the Budget Bureau and William Howard Taft became the chief justice. After that, however, Harding began running into problems. His cronies from Ohio, who had helped to get him elected, wanted their share of the political spoils. Along with a few others, like New Mexico Senator Albert Fall, they were given the major offices in the new administration. The result was that most of the people in government knew one another and got along well. They were dubbed the "Ohio Gang" and, theoretically, it should have made for an efficient government. Instead, it spelled disaster for the administration.

The Ohio Gang almost systematically began using their newfound powers to rob the government. It still remains unclear how much, if anything, Harding himself knew about his friend's illegal activities. Likely, though, it wasn't much. Political boss Harry Daughtery, who got Harding elected to the Senate and accepted a position as one of the Ohio Gang, always considered Harding a "dimwit." He later admitted that he pushed Harding into the presidency only because "he looked presidential." Harding's intelligence (or lack thereof) may have been the reason he got so much support from his political pals—they knew how easy it would be to get away with illicit activities once their friend was in office!

As mentioned earlier, Harding was aware of his own incompetence and bemoaned the fact that he had no business being in the Oval Office. He was bewildered by taxes, foreign affairs and the economy, and only found reassurance from the letters that he received from the public. He spent an inordinate amount of time answering mail that should have been handled by his staff. He also liked greeting visitors to the White House, shaking hands and chatting for hours. His greatest flaw was his chronic need to be liked. People took advantage of it, especially his "friends" who knew that he would never offend them by interfering in their business. His friends were important and he sought their approval by filling high government posts with them, playing poker in the White House with them and providing them with Prohibition-era booze.

He also allowed them to rape and pillage the country, whether he knew what was happening or not.

Harry Daughtery, Harding's political guide, was named to the position of attorney general. When Harding was warned against making this appointment, he had a quick reply: "Harry Daughtery has been my best friend since the beginning of this whole thing... He tells me that he wants to be attorney general and by God, he will be attorney general!"

Daughtery set up an influence-peddling office at the Department of Justice and eventually became the subject of two congressional investigations. After he resigned, he was indicted two times for malfeasance while in office, but only because the statute of limitations had expired for the real charge of accepting bribes. Jess Smith, a personal aide to the attorney general, was accused of destroying papers that would have harmed Daughtery. No one knows for sure what was on them because Smith committed suicide soon after.

Another of Harding's close friends was Colonel Charles Forbes, who became the director of the Veterans Bureau. Forbes convinced Harding to transfer the planning and construction of all future military hospitals from the army to his department, along with the authority to purchase and administer veterans' supplies. During his time in office, Forbes profited lavishly from kickbacks and he even directed underground alcohol and drug distribution. He was convicted of fraud and bribery and drew a two-year sentence. Charles Cramer, an aide to Charles Forbes, committed suicide when the scandal was uncovered. Forbes was convicted of fraud and bribery and received a two-year sentence. Thomas Miller, head of the Office of Alien Property, was also convicted of receiving bribes.

But there was no one who did as much damage to Harding's reputation as his good friend, Secretary of the Interior Albert Fall, a passionate White House poker player and the architect of the great Teapot Dome swindle. Harding had befriended the senator from New Mexico when he himself was a new senator from Ohio. After he was elected president, he appointed Fall to his cabinet. He had no idea that this appointment would lead to one of the greatest scandals of the time, shaking the nation for years after Harding's death.

Albert Fall owned a sprawling ranch in New Mexico and was an outspoken opponent of the government setting aside land for conservation, including a number of oil reserves that were controlled by the U.S. Navy. It was one of those reserves, Teapot Dome in Wyoming (named for its resemblance to a giant sandstone teapot), that lent its name to the scandal.

Senator Albert Fall. *National Archives.*

Fall managed to get the control of several oil reserves, including Teapot Dome, transferred from the control of the navy to the Department of the Interior. He then leased them out to the private interests of Harry Sinclair and E.L. Doheny, two major oil producers. The leases were granted without competitive bidding, which was not illegal, but Fall received "loans" from both men amounting to about $400,000 in exchange for licenses to secretly plunder the reserves. The "loans" were never documented or acknowledged, which, of course, made them bribes. In 1931, Fall became the first member of a presidential cabinet to be sent to prison.

Rumors circulated about graft and corruption within the administration. Harding started to show the effects of constant strain and his health suffered, just as it had years before when he checked into a sanatorium to rest. This time, though, there was no getting out of the spotlight. He was quoted as saying: "My God, this is a hell of a job! I have no trouble with my enemies... But my damn friends; they're the ones that keep me walking the floor nights."

Harding was under a lot of stress, but there always seemed to be someone around to help him relieve it—someone of the female persuasion, that is. Even before he came to the White House, Harding had a reputation for involving himself in extramarital affairs. Some of them were said to be short-lived, but at least two of them were extended unions that went on for years.

Harding's first mistress was a young woman named Carrie Phillips, the wife of a longtime friend, James Phillips, owner of the local department store, the Uhler-Phillips Company. The daring Carrie, who was ten years younger than Harding, would often strut down the street in front of the Hardings' Marion home, much to the anger of "The Duchess." On one occasion, witnesses spotted Carrie talking to Harding from the sidewalk in front of the house. Harding was standing on the front porch. Suddenly, Florence appeared from inside of the house and starting throwing things at Carrie, including a feather duster, a wastebasket and then a piano stool. It was not until this heavy, wooden object was tossed in her direction that Carrie finally retreated up the street. Even then, she did not do it quietly. She had the nerve to blow Harding a kiss and then march away.

The Phillips affair ended badly. Carrie demanded that Harding divorce his wife and marry her—just before he was elected president. With all of the love letters that he had written in her possession, she blackmailed him, even though he had already given her a Cadillac and offered her a "hush money" payment of $5,000 per year.

Harding found himself in a predicament with the Republican National Party because he had never disclosed the affair to party officials. Once they learned of it, it was too late to try and find another nominee. In order to avoid a scandal, the Republican National Committee, through campaign manager Albert Lasker, paid Carrie $20,000 and sent her and her husband on a trip to Japan. This got them safely out of the country before the election took place. Carrie's continued monthly payments made her the first, and perhaps only person known to have successfully extorted money from a major political party.

Harding was also documented to have had an affair with Nan Britton, the daughter of Harding's friend, Dr. Britton of Marion. Nan first developed a crush on Harding when she was a teenager, and reportedly was a virgin the first time they made love. In a book that Nan later wrote about the affair, she claimed that she and Harding conceived a daughter when he was still a senator. The daughter, Elizabeth Ann, was born on October 22, 1919. Harding never met the girl, but he did pay large amounts of child support for her care.

He and Nan were said to have continued the affair after he became president in 1921. When Nan visited the White House, they allegedly slipped away to a small coat closet for a rendezvous. The story goes that they were once nearly caught in the act by "The Duchess." Five minutes after they entered the closet, Florence showed up, searching for where they had disappeared to. She demanded that the secret service agent who was guarding the closet door abandon his post and get out of her way. When he refused, she ran around the corner to enter the closet through another room. The agent knocked loudly on the door to alert the president, who got Nan out of the building. Harding had just enough time to get to his desk and pretend to be working before Florence found him.

After Harding's death, Nan tried unsuccessfully to sue his estate on behalf of Elizabeth Ann. Under cross-examination by Harding heirs' attorney, Nan's testimony was riddled with inconsistencies, and she lost the case. She was later married and her new husband adopted Elizabeth Ann. The girl went on to marry and raise her own family. She stayed away from press coverage throughout most of her life and always turned down interviews about Harding. Elizabeth Ann died in Oregon in 2005.

Her death marked an end to a controversial part of Warren G. Harding's life. Speculation about his affairs did not end with his death—and speculation about the facts behind his death has not yet ended today.

Harding's final days began with news that the Senate was debating the formation of a special committee to investigate the leasing of navy oil reserve lands to private companies. It's unlikely that Harding knew the full extent of his friend Albert Fall's duplicity in this affair but regardless, the president put all of his efforts and resources behind a move to defeat the creation of such a committee. He knew that if investigations were started, it would mean disaster for his administration, and possibly impeachment for himself.

To raise the president's spirits, a cross-country trip (dubbed a "Voyage of Understanding") was planned. During this trip, he became the first president to visit Alaska. The rumors of corruption in his administration were beginning to circulate wider and wider in Washington by the time he departed in June 1923, and Harding was profoundly shocked by one long message that he received while in Alaska. It apparently detailed illegal activities that had been previously unknown to him. Reporters later asked a depressed looking Harding what was wrong and he was said to have asked them what a president could do when he found out that his friends had betrayed him.

During the trip, Harding traveled in Alaska and Canada and then as his train was passing through Seattle, he became ill. Surgeon General Charles Sawyer diagnosed his ailment as food poisoning. He gave the final speech of his life to a large crowd at the University of Washington and then took a train heading south. On July 29, Harding checked into the Palace Hotel. He developed pneumonia and had a fever of one hundred and two degrees. On August 1, his fever broke and he began to breathe more comfortably. Believing that he was actually getting better, he made plans to go fishing the next day.

Then, he died. On August 2, he died of either a heart attack or a stroke. The formal announcement in the newspapers the following day stated: "A stroke of apoplexy was the cause of death."

According to Mrs. Harding, he had been feeling much better the previous evening and she had been reading aloud a flattering article about him that had appeared in the *Saturday Evening Post*. Harding supposedly said: "That's good. Go on, read some more." Those became his last words.

His eyes were closed when Florence finished reading the article and she left the room, assuming that the president was asleep. Later, nurse Ruth Powderly came in, saw his face twitch, his mouth drop open and his head roll to the side. From her statement, doctors concluded that he had suffered a stroke.

Many believe that this is where the mystery started.

Mrs. Harding refused to allow an autopsy on her husband. As it happened, California, where Harding's death occurred, did not have a mandatory autopsy law. Not surprisingly, with all of the stories of scandal around the administration, several rumors were started. One story stated that the president, already depressed and fearing impeachment, committed suicide. Another claimed that Mrs. Harding poisoned him, either to prevent the humiliation of scandal over the wrongdoings of the Ohio Gang or because she wanted revenge for his numerous indiscretions.

The claim that Florence murdered her husband was enhanced by the publication of a book called *The Mysterious Death of Warren G. Harding* by Gaston Means, a convicted swindler. According to Means, he worked as a private detective and had been employed by Mrs. Harding for various questionable projects, including breaking into Nan Britton's apartment to steal some love letters that the president had written. Means claimed that Florence often confided in him and that she had described to him Harding's final moments—just after she had given him poison.

Although most historians have dismissed the idea that Mrs. Harding murdered her husband, what really may have killed him remains unknown. The lack of an autopsy managed to prevent any definitive answer, but the truth was, no one really made much of an effort to find one. Had Harding lived, he almost certainly would have been impeached and removed from office, and no one wanted to keep trying to dig up dirt on a dead man. With other scandals to take its place, the importance of Warren G. Harding's death faded over time. In the end, his passing, like his presidency, left little impression on American history.

THE PRESIDENT'S WHISKEY

Franklin Pierce of New Hampshire may have been the first president elected on the strength of his propaganda rather than for his skills in office. Pierce was a close friend of the great poet and novelist Nathaniel Hawthorne. As the 1852 presidential campaign approached, Hawthorne wrote a flowery biography about Pierce that was designed to make people think they would be crazy not to vote for him. It said everything about Franklin Pierce but the truth—that he was a nice looking loser. Harry Truman once said of him: "Pierce was the best looking president the White House ever had, but as a president, he ranks with Buchanan and Calvin Coolidge." Regardless, Hawthorne's book helped him win the election.

Author Michael Farquhar describes Pierce as a "small, weak man" who was accused, perhaps unfairly, of cowardice during the Mexican War. He was married to a reclusive and very eccentric woman who dressed all in black and spent each day writing letters to her dead son.

Pierce turned to drink to cope with the pressures of life in the White House. At first, he drank a little and then it became a lot. His drinking became so bad that stories of his escapades often made the rounds in Washington. One night, it was said that a policeman arrested a drunk for stampeding his horse down city streets, almost running over a woman. The "drunk" turned out to be the president of the United States, and the charges against him were quickly dropped.

Pierce eventually died from cirrhosis of the liver, earning him a unique spot as the hardest drinking of all of our American presidents.

Our Fattest President

There is no question that William Howard Taft was the largest president to ever serve our country. Taft himself, was not unaware of the fact, and much was spoken and written about his corpulence during the time that he was in office. In addition to his size—or likely because of it—Taft had difficulty staying awake.

It's very possible that Taft suffered from what is known today as obstructive sleep apnea, a condition that causes the throat to close down while a person sleeps, causing them to stop breathing. Sufferers from this condition are often plagued with heart trouble, impotence and a tendency to fall asleep during inopportune times, like when driving or in Taft's case, during cabinet meetings. Because sleep apnea does not allow the sufferer to sleep soundly (they are constantly in a state of wakefulness, struggling for breath), they are always tired. This condition seems to affect men more than women because men, when they gain weight, tend to put on pounds in the neck. The added flesh constricts the throat and aggravates the condition. Today, surgery and breathing machines can help those who have sleep apnea, but in Taft's day there was nothing to be done aside from losing weight, which the president had no interest in doing.

Taft's size and condition contributed to his habit of falling asleep at terrible times, such as in the front row of a state funeral, riding in an open car during his campaign or while being briefed by his White House staff. It was often embarrassing for Taft and for his beleaguered staff, who would do almost anything to keep the president awake.

Staff members recalled incidents where Taft was simply unable to stay awake. After dinner with cabinet members one evening, he called for music to be played on the Victrola, but he fell asleep

William Howard Taft, our nation's fattest president. *Library of Congress.*

during the first song. When he woke up, he called for another record, but then dozed off again before it could be played. Attorney General George Wickersham called for a particularly loud song to be played and commented: "It will wake anyone but a dead man." The song failed to rouse the slumbering president and Wickersham had one last comment to make: "He must be dead."

One night, while attending the opera, Taft aide Archie Butt tried to keep the president awake through the first act but he was unable to do so. He kept nudging him as the intermission grew closer and closer as he did not want the audience to see that Taft had been snoring through a command performance. Mercifully, the president awoke with seconds to spare, never realizing that it had been the sharp toe of Archie's shoe that had prodded him to consciousness.

As mentioned, Taft knew that he had a weight problem. He wrote to his wife, Helen: "I will make a conscientious effort to lose flesh. I am convinced that this undue drowsiness is due to the accumulation of flesh." But Taft never lost the weight. After he left office as the fattest president in history, he went on to become the fattest United States chief justice in history.

Taft did have a sense of humor about his immense size, however. He often liked to tell a story from his days as the governor general of the Philippines. He had sent a telegram to Secretary of War Elihu Root and said: "Took long horseback ride today; feeling fine."

Root immediately wrote back: "How is the horse?"

The Traitorous President

Only a handful of American presidents go on to make a name for themselves after retiring from office. Most of them return home to write a book, see a library named in their honor, try to rescue their reputations or something else of a quiet nature. Only one U.S. president did something so strange that it had never been done before and has never been done since—he went to work for an enemy country.

Traitorous President John Tyler. *National Archives.*

John Tyler was the first of what has been referred to as "accidental presidents." He inherited the office after the death of William Henry

Harrison in 1841. It had been obnoxiousness that killed Harrison. He had made a long and tedious inauguration speech in a cold rain and was dead from pneumonia a month later.

After serving out Harrison's remaining term—and coming close to being impeached—Tyler retired to his Virginia estate, where he lived quietly until the start of the Civil War fifteen years later. As a loyal Virginia man, Tyler took up the Confederate cause, backed the state's succession from the Union, and was elected to the Confederacy's House of Representatives in 1861.

He did not have much time to betray his country. He died just before taking his seat, depriving himself of the opportunity to be the first U.S. president to serve two countries—and the first to be a traitor to the one that put him into the White House.

THE VICE PRESIDENT'S MISTRESSES

Richard Mentor Johnson was perhaps the most unconventional, at least when it came to women, of all of the men who served as the second to the president. While his quirks might not seem as strange today, they were certainly controversial at the time. Johnson was vice president under Martin Van Buren, and while the Kentuckian never married, he certainly ran through a string of women in his time.

He always believed that his love life had been ruined by his mother. It's likely that he would have lived an ordinary married life if she had allowed him to marry the New England schoolteacher that he fell in love with as a young man. She refused to allow the union to take place, however, and Johnson was permanently marked by this decision. He promised that, in time, he would have his revenge.

When Johnson's father died a few years later, the still angry son decided to make his mother regret her actions. As part of his inheritance from his father's estate, Johnson received a young female slave, Julia Chinn, who had been on their plantation since she was a child. Johnson decided to take the girl as his mistress. He put her in charge of his home, introduced her into society as his wife and had several children with her. After he was elected to the United States Senate, he took Julia to Washington and referred to her in public as his wife. When people refused to accept her and rebelled against her presence at society parties, Johnson himself refused to attend.

Julia died during a cholera epidemic in 1833 and Johnson decided not to spend the rest of his life as a bachelor. Despite the fact that he was in the national spotlight and was mentioned as a possible presidential candidate, he began taking other slaves as his mistresses. Even after he was elected vice president by the Senate in 1837, he continued to keep these women in his home and introduced them as his wives.

Johnson was an unusual man, which was obvious to the people of Washington at the time. He never felt that he was exploiting these women because that was simply not something that most slave owners thought about at the time. However, he did feel that he possessed a good sense of personal morality—when one of his mistresses proved unfaithful, he put her up for sale and took her sister as his mistress instead.

The (Almost) Death of a President

President Chester A. Arthur. *Library of Congress.*

Although it's commonly accepted today, the American people were kept in the dark for many years concerning the health problems of beloved president Franklin Delano Roosevelt. Most did not know that he was unable to stand without assistance, and photographs and newsreels were careful not to show him in his wheelchair. But one of the best kept secrets of the Oval Office was that one president spent a good part of his administration very close to death!

Although the public was unaware of it at the time, President Chester A. Arthur was terminally ill with Bright's Disease and spent his last years in office knowing that he could very well die before his term ended. Because his advisors had concerns about creating an unstable political and economic situation, they reasoned that the public should not be told about the president's health problems. It had been bad enough that Arthur had stepped into office after the assassination of James Garfield, but to announce that the new president might not live out his term would seriously damage his ability as a leader.

Instead of releasing the news, all references to illness were buried and the secret was closely guarded. President Arthur and his staff filled the White House with parties and laughter, and pretended that nothing was wrong.

Although expected to step down at the end of his term, Arthur made a feeble attempt to gain his party's nomination for a second time. His heart wasn't in it, though. He knew that the more active he was, the greater the chance of succumbing to the disease. In the end, he managed to survive his four years in office, and did not die from the disease until a year and a half later in 1886.

THEODORE ROOSEVELT—BLACKMAILER?

The story that President Theodore Roosevelt was using the Secret Service to dig up information on members of Congress quickly made the rounds of Washington's political circles. Was there any truth to the rumor? No one knew but Congress believed it, and in the end that turned out to be all that mattered.

It was a story often repeated in congressmen's offices, at dinner parties and in Washington saloons—the president was a blackmailer. According to the rumor, it was all because of several important votes that were coming up. Looking for every advantage that he could get, Roosevelt sent the Secret Service out to try and dig up some dirt on key members of Congress. In particular, he had ordered them to find out which members frequented Washington's whorehouses! When he had that information in hand, he could force congressmen to adopt the administration's line on every vote. If they didn't, news about their shady activities would be splashed across the front pages of the newspapers.

There was nothing to say that such a story was true—but it was not too far-fetched either. During the previous session, Congress had passed an amendment that required the Secret Service to limit its investigations to the activities of the executive branch. Roosevelt was now asking for this amendment to be repealed. The president openly stated that the Secret Service should be able to investigate anyone. Even, he added, members of Congress. Congress was in a panic. Was Roosevelt trying to put together a private police force that could blackmail members of the government? Some members believed that he was.

Overall, though, the majority of Congress saw the story for just what it was—a rumor. Cleverly, though, Roosevelt refused to comment on it one

President Theodore Roosevelt—was he trying to blackmail members of Congress? *National Archives.*

way or another, perhaps deliberately planting a seed of doubt in some congressmen's minds. They must have been wondering as they took a drink, slipped away to the house of a mistress or joined a group of friends at a local whorehouse—who was watching them?

Roosevelt's insinuations may have had many wondering just what he was up to but it's possible that planting seeds of doubt in their minds may have backfired on him. Many of the legislators became so worked up over what Roosevelt *might* be doing that they decided to censure him, just two months before the end of his term. It was only the second time in history (aside from the impeachment of Andrew Johnson) that Congress censured a president. The first time had been when Congress censured Andrew Jackson during the controversy over the Bank of the United States. Jackson's censure ended up expunged from the records of Congress through the efforts of Thomas Hart Benton.

The censure of Theodore Roosevelt—over a rumor—was never removed.

WAS THE PRESIDENT'S WIFE A BIGAMIST?

The followers of Andrew Jackson cried foul after the election of 1824. Just days after it had ended in victory for John Quincy Adams, they were demanding an investigation. Jackson had received a plurality of the popular and electoral votes, but he fell short of the majority, which sent the election to the House of Representatives. In the House, Henry Clay's support for Adams tipped the scale. When the smoke cleared, Adams selected Clay as his secretary of state and Jackson supporters accused both men of a "corrupt bargain."

Four years later, Jackson's men were looking to even the score and the election was one of the nastiest in American history. Jackson's supporters denounced Adams as a gambler (he had purchased a billiard table for the White House) and a pimp (the story, which was not true but was often told, claimed that while Adams was a diplomat in Russia he had supplied American virgins to the czar).

Adams' supporters responded with equally vile accusations. They denounced Jackson's reputation as a military hero by painting him as a crazed lunatic who might explode into violence at any time. The fact that Jackson had fought in eight duels and a deadly tavern brawl didn't help his reputation, nor did the execution of six soldiers who attempted to start a mutiny during the Creek Indian campaign in 1813–1814. Americans could live with a president with a taste for blood, though, so these claims were not taken too seriously. What became the most widely circulated charge against Jackson was that he was an adulterer and that his wife, Rachel, was a bigamist.

This was the charge that presented the most difficult problem for Jackson, mostly because—at least technically—it was the truth.

Once this charge was placed before the public, Jackson's supporters put together an eighteen-man committee to gather evidence and present his side of the story. A big part of Jackson's story was an eyewitness account by a man named John Overton, who was present for much of what took place.

Around 1787, Overton became a boarder in the Kentucky home of the widow Robards. Also living in the house was her son, Lewis Robards, and his wife, Rachel Robards, who later became Rachel Jackson. The marriage of Lewis and Rachel was a disaster from the beginning. Lewis Robards was a backward, irritable man who was always suspicious of his wife and the motives of everyone around him. Rachel was just the opposite, often attending parties, dancing and riding horses. Everything that she did seemed to bring out her husband's jealous streak. At least once Overton had to intervene in a violent

Andrew Jackson. *Library of Congress.*

fight between the husband and wife. Eventually, Lewis and Rachel, along with Overton, moved to Tennessee, near Nashville, and began boarding with Rachel's mother, the widow Donelson.

This was when Andrew Jackson entered the story. Like Overton, he was a young frontier lawyer and he also became a boarder at the widow Donelson's house. It seemed almost inevitable that two hot-tempered men like Jackson and Lewis Robards would clash. When Robards found Jackson talking to Rachel one day—a completely innocent conversation, Overton assured the investigation board—Robards was enraged. Jackson tried to reason with him but the other man refused to listen. He left the house in a rage, moved back to Kentucky and vowed to never live with Rachel again.

But some time in the fall of 1790, he changed his mind, or at least this was the story that went around in Nashville at the time. When Rachel heard that her husband intended to take her back to Kentucky, even if it required force, Rachel was understandably upset. She decided to leave Nashville before Robards arrived and flee down the Mississippi to Natchez, where she had friends who would protect her.

According to Overton, Jackson was upset by this latest development, but not, he emphasized again, because he had done anything wrong. So Jackson decided to help out by joining the party that was going down the river. It was dangerous Indian country that they would be passing through and he wanted to offer whatever protection he could.

Overton recalled that in the late winter or early spring of 1791, Jackson and Rachel set off for Natchez. Jackson did not remain there. By May, he was back in Nashville, where he learned that the legislature had granted Robards a divorce. (At that time, divorce was so rare that it required a legislative act.) Jackson then hurried back to Natchez, where he married Rachel in the summer of 1791. They lived together there for a short time, and then in the fall returned to Nashville together.

The story should have ended there, but it didn't. In December 1793, more than two years after they had gotten married, the Jacksons were horrified to learn that Robards had not gotten a divorce after all. The legislature had merely passed an act that enabled Robards to take Rachel to court. He didn't get around to doing this for two years and since Jackson and Rachel had been living together during that time, Robards had no trouble convincing a jury that she was guilty of adultery. Since she had been married to Jackson during this period, she was also guilty of the worse crime of bigamy.

Overton emphasized the fact that Rachel's "guilt" was merely a technicality. When Jackson and Rachel had married in 1791, they truly believed that she was divorced and the crime of bigamy had been an unintentional one. When they learned that their original marriage was not valid, they immediately got married again.

This was the story that the committee released to the public during the 1828 presidential campaign and while it was clearly told from Jackson's side (the Adams' camp called them the "Whitewashing Committee"), it included a great deal of supporting evidence. But there were also a lot of holes in the story...

Many were skeptical as to how Jackson, a lawyer, could have rushed into a marriage without actually checking to see if the legislative act that allowed the marriage was actually valid. Also, how could the Jacksons have lived together for two years without any suspicion about the divorce? Communications on the frontier were slow and inaccurate, though, so an error of that sort was by no means out of the question.

The story stood for years, but questions do occasionally surface. Author Robert Remini, who wrote a major biography of Andrew Jackson, was skeptical of the Overton narrative. First, he wondered about Jackson's decision to accompany Rachel to Natchez. He thought that someone else could have surely accompanied her down the river besides the man who had been accused of being her lover. Couldn't one of her ten brothers or brothers-in-law have protected her on the journey? Or couldn't they have protected her in Nashville? Remini felt the story didn't make sense and that Jackson was already in love with Rachel, and that he planned the trip as a way to provoke Robards into filing for divorce. This was not an immoral plan. Rachel was trapped in a horrible, violent marriage and this may have been the only way out that she could find. Regardless, it was not the "innocent" plan that Overton described to the committee.

The author also found some odd things regarding the wedding itself. According to Natchez records of the time, Jackson and Rachel arrived in January 1790, not 1791 as Overton claimed. If this is the case, then the couple was married, or at least living together, for months before the divorce proceedings were started, let alone allegedly completed.

And the charges made in 1827 that "General Jackson prevailed upon the wife of Lewis Robards to desert her husband and live with himself in the character of a wife" were actually true.

But this did not make Jackson any more forgiving toward those who dared to speak of them. The attacks during the campaign were not the first time that Jackson had defended the honor of his wife. He was nearly insane with rage when anyone spoke against her and their marital confusion made her a target for many of his political enemies, including the first governor of Tennessee, John Sevier.

After a series of political clashes, Sevier verbally attacked Jackson, who was then a judge on the Tennessee Superior Court, outside of a Knoxville courthouse in 1803. He taunted Jackson: "I know of no great services you have tendered to the country except taking a trip to Natchez with another man's wife!"

Jackson was infuriated that Sevier dared to even speak of Rachel. Pistols were drawn and shots were fired, but neither man was wounded. They were quickly separated, but Jackson, still furious, challenged Sevier to a formal duel. When the governor hedged, Jackson took out an advertisement in the *Tennessee Gazette* and called him a coward.

When the two eventually met on the field of honor, they immediately started insulting each other and Jackson rushed at the governor with his stick. Sevier drew his sword, which frightened his horse, and the animal rode away with his dueling pistols still in the saddle bag. Jackson decided to take advantage of the situation and he drew his own pistol as Sevier ducked for cover behind a tree. Seeing his father in danger, Sevier's son drew his pistol on Jackson, while Jackson's second pointed his weapon at the son. At a stalemate, and realizing how ridiculous the situation had become, the parties left the field. They remained lifelong enemies.

But harsh words between two politicians were not the same as seeing stories of bigamy in national newspapers. It's interesting to note the difference between what happened in Nashville in the early 1790s and what happened in Washington in the late 1820s. Times had changed, but then the frontier view of the Jackson marriage had rarely been one of disapproval. Frontier life called for all sorts of improvisation and the Jacksons were hardly unique in making the best of a bad situation. The national morals of the 1820s, though, were much more prudish, and the situation was definitely colored by the political spin that Adams' supporters added to the story.

No matter what the public really thought about the accusations, Rachel was bothered by them. Although she was shielded from much of the campaign rhetoric, she came upon some pamphlets during a shopping trip right after the election. What she read shocked her, and many felt that it contributed to the heart attack that she suffered soon after. She died just before she was to accompany her husband to the White House.

This made Jackson's victory over Adams a bittersweet one. His beloved Rachel was dead and he was convinced that the slanders against her were the cause. He exclaimed at her grave site: "May God Almighty forgive her murderers, as I know she forgave them. I never can."

Andrew Jackson never forgot the attacks on his wife and they had a great impact on his presidency. When the wife of Vice President John Calhoun refused to call on the notoriously promiscuous wife of a cabinet member, Jackson saw the attacks on the man's wife as being comparable to the attacks on Rachel. Because of this, Jackson came to her defense. The incident became a major scandal, occupying a great amount of cabinet meeting time, and it led to a rift between Jackson and Calhoun that eventually made it possible for Martin Van Buren, not Calhoun, to succeed Jackson in office.

The vehement attacks on Rachel Jackson, and the charges and countercharges that followed, also led to change in American politics. Politics had always been messy, personal and nasty, but by 1828 it was much easier for the press and the parties involved to spread negative stories about the candidates. Things were only going to get worse in the future, securing the idea that politics was not a game for those who were faint of heart!

6.

Bloody Washington

Strange Tales of Crime, Murder & Death

It is human nature for us to love a mystery. We all love to be intrigued by the mysterious and tantalized by the idea of something that cannot be solved. For this reason, murder mysteries, courtroom dramas and books about crime and wicked cities have been immensely popular for decades. We love to question, to wonder and be baffled by those things that we believe to be unexplained. Of course, most fictional mysteries are usually solved by the intrepid detective in the closing pages of the book or the last reel of the film, but what of mysteries that cannot be solved? What of real-life mysteries for which no explanation exists?

The history of Washington has been checkered by such enigmas and puzzles. In unsuspecting places, we find tales of crimes for which all clues have vanished over the passage of time. In other cases, we know the identity of the killer, but his motives remain mysterious.

In the pages ahead, it is not my intention to glorify these killers or their crimes, but merely to examine them as historical poof that the "good old days" weren't always good. The specter of crime in those days, as it does now, often lurked around every corner.

The Washington Vampire

Perhaps one of the strangest stories to ever be told in Washington can be traced to a 1923 account in the *Washington Post*, one of the capital's leading newspapers. A writer named Gorman Hendricks was given quite a lot of space for some unusual reports about a vampire that had been stalking Washington since the 1850s. This "creature of the night" had been preying on her old northeast Washington neighborhood until just before the story appeared in the newspaper. At that time, her burial vault, located a short distance east of the sprawling Brentwood estate had been "dismantled and the body entombed there subjected to ghoulish desecration."

Could such a story be true? Many in Washington believe that it was!

The story of the Washington Vampire began not with the 1923 newspaper story, but in the 1850s, when a young woman fell in love with a handsome European prince who was visiting this country. The young woman in question was a daughter of a respected local family and lived in the neighborhood where Gallaudet College is now located. The young woman's father, being well-known in local political circles, took her along to a party one evening where she met the prince. She had no way of knowing, the account stated, that this man was a vampire until he got her alone that evening. Her pale body was discovered the next morning, drained of blood. The strange prince was reportedly never seen again.

A funeral service was held for the young woman and she was laid to rest in the family's burial vault, which was located behind their home. But, having been bitten by a vampire herself, the girl was doomed to rise from her grave and seek out her own victims.

The first terrifying encounter with this new vampire occurred a short time after the young woman's funeral. A local laborer was making his way home by cutting through an old family cemetery when he spotted "a white-robed figure of a woman floating through a sealed vault." No one believed his story until the lifeless body of a stable hand was found a few weeks later. Two vivid red bite marks were found on the man's throat, and remembering the laborer's story, the people in the neighborhood were filled with panic. They were so scared that the vampire might return that they hired two heavily armed men to spend the night in front of the burial vault. This watch was maintained for many nights before the vampire put in another appearance.

On the night of April 22, the two guards were startled by the sound of what seemed to be the squeak of rusty hinges. They claimed they were too scared to react as a figure in white crept out and "glided through the woods in the direction of the mansion." The men did not stay around long enough to see if she slipped inside. They ran from the cemetery and went straight to the home of the man who hired them and told the neighbors their incredible news.

The next morning, long after the sun had burned the darkness from the sky, a small group of locals cautiously ventured to the old estate to investigate. Inside of the tomb, they found that the "huge stone slab that had been over the coffin was displaced." They claimed that the girl was lying in the coffin, and although she had been dead by this time for many months, she looked just as she did when she died. Her skin was pale but had not decomposed and her hair appeared to have grown. She looked completely ordinary except for the fact that "sharp wolf-like fangs" protruded over her bottom lip. The sight of the girl brought gasps from the assembled group and they fled from the cemetery. They took the time to replace the stone over the girl's coffin but nothing was done to stop her from leaving her grave again. Not surprisingly, tales of her nocturnal journeys continued.

A few months later, another encounter with the vampire made local news. A man was walking near the old graveyard and was terrified by the girl as she floated through the trees surrounding the cemetery. The man told a newspaper reporter that she was laughing manically and that her eyes gleamed with "hell-fire." The man was so frightened that he never recovered from it. He died a short time later but his throat was apparently intact.

According to the account, neighbors of the family who lived in the mansion began harassing them to leave the area. Perhaps they hoped that with her family gone, the vampire might follow after them. The family moved out but the stories continued to be told. Those who lived nearby frequently saw a wraith in a white dress as she prowled the graveyard and the dark streets nearby. The house where her family had lived was abandoned and sat empty for years. The tales of the creature spread throughout the area and no one wanted to live in the so-called "vampire house." The mansion remained deserted for many years, slowly crumbling into ruin, until a family that was unfamiliar with the old stories finally purchased it in the 1920s. They did not stay unfamiliar with them for long…

Soon after they took up residence in the old mansion, the vampire returned. Apparently, the lure of fresh blood was something she was unable to resist. The new occupants reported a horrible figure "gazing in the window of an upper room" and they quickly moved out.

Neighbors, now generations after the original neighbors of the "vampire house," found themselves terrified again. Having believed they were rid of the monster that had plagued their parents, grandparents and relatives, they shunned the property once more, avoiding it during the daytime and especially at night. When thunderstorms rolled into the area, they refused to go outside at all.

Finally, in 1923, they decided that something had to be done.

According to Gorman Hendricks, who wrote his vampire article for the *Washington Post* soon after the vigilantes ventured out to the graveyard for the last time, he described the door of the crypt as hanging on "rusty hinges" and added that the "hand of time has obliterated the name." He wrote that "large sections of broken sandstone that once covered the tombs of the dead lie about the dank vault given over to the creatures that creep and crawl."

Hendricks did not go into detail as to what occurred in the crypt that night, but whatever it was, he described it as "ghoulish desecration," leading many to believe that perhaps a stake was driven into the vampire's heart. Regardless, the woman in white was no longer reported wandering the streets of northeast Washington, peering in windows and terrifying the local populace. The vampire could now apparently, after nearly seventy years, finally rest in peace.

What can we make of a story like this? Was the entire thing just a hoax? Or was there really something sinister taking place in the northeast part of the city that people attributed to a "vampire"? Whether this creature had supernatural origins or not, the accounts of it make for some of the strangest tales of crime and horror in the history of Washington.

THE STRANGE DEATH OF MARIAN "CLOVER" ADAMS

"The poor unfortunate Mrs. Adams…."

This is how neighbors in Washington referred to the untimely death of Marian Cooper Adams, and they whispered of strange things when they spoke of her gravesite in the old Rock Creek Cemetery off North Capitol Street. The gravesite bore no inscription and no date. Only a silent sentinel that sculptor Augustus Saint-Gaudens called "Grief" marked the place where she was laid to rest.

Marian Adams' grave is a mystery, as was much of her life and her death. Marian, who was known by the affectionate nickname of "Clover," was a well-educated, intelligent and beautiful woman who met her husband, the author Henry Adams, in London. It was not love at first sight between them but they shared many interests and the relationship, however strange it turned out to be, slowly blossomed into love. As Marian discovered, falling in love with Henry Adams could be a daunting and intimidating thing.

Henry Adams was born in Boston on February 16, 1838, the fourth of seven children of Charles Francis and Abigail Brooks Adams. Henry's mother was the daughter of one of Boston's wealthiest men. His father, a respected diplomat, was the son of John Quincy Adams, sixth president of the United States, and the grandson of John Adams, the second president. Henry grew up in a household that contained Boston's largest private library and in which politics played an active role.

Author Henry Adams. *National Archives.*

Henry graduated from Harvard in 1858 and then traveled to Germany, where he intended to study law at the University of Berlin. When he discovered that his German was not fluent enough for his studies, he toured Europe for two years, sending reports of his travels to a Boston newspaper.

Henry returned to America in 1860 and became a private secretary for his father, who had been elected to Congress. He also arranged to act as a Washington correspondent for a Boston newspaper. But the two men's plans were altered in March 1861 when President Lincoln appointed Charles Francis Adams as minister to Great Britain. By the time that Charles and Henry had arrived in England, the Civil War had broken out. Henry thought of seeking a commission, but his older brother, Charles, already in the army, urged him to remain in England and advance the Union cause as a writer. He filed many reports in the *New York Times* during this period and advanced his education on politics, economics and science. He published a number of important articles, including three long and promising pieces for the influential *North American Review.*

Henry returned to the United States in 1868 and settled in Washington, where he reported on the political scene for several newspapers. He became a noted critic and social commentator, and his brilliant and acerbic articles soon made him famous. In the autumn of 1870, he reluctantly left Washington for Boston to become the editor of the *North American Review* and an assistant professor of history at Harvard. He would remain at Harvard, writing some of his monumental histories of America, until he and his wife settled in Washington several years later.

It was in 1872 that Henry and Marian met in London, and this began a period in Henry's life that many historians are still puzzling over today.

The courtship between Henry and Marian seemed to be progressing nicely but Adams wrote a strange letter to his friend, English nobleman Charles M. Gaskell, just three months before the wedding:

> *She is very open to instruction. We shall improve her. She dresses badly. She decidedly has humor and will appreciate our wit. She has enough money to be quite independent... I don't want you to marry though. One of us surely should remain single for the good of all.*

In the time before the wedding, Adams wrote several letters to Gaskell, each assuring him that his marriage would not affect their friendship. Author Sarah Booth Conroy stated: "Henry's actions and writings may be interpreted in many and varied ways to suggest homosexuality, bisexuality, asexuality or impotence." There was plenty of gossip that swirled around at the time, but historians today can only speculate about what it all meant. What is known is that Henry and Clover were married for thirteen years, and during much of that time she worked as his research assistant and perfected her interest in photography, a hobby to which Henry had introduced her.

Henry and Clover lived in Boston for a time and then moved to Washington. Here, they rented a house near 16th and H Street NW, which was owned by famous art collector W.W. Cochran, who lived just down the block. Lincoln biographer John Hay became Henry's closest friend. Clover got along well with Hay's wife, Clara, and together with friend Clarence King, they formed a mock secret society that they called "The Five of Hearts."

Over the next several seemingly uneventful years, Henry continued his writing and Clover continued her pursuit of photography, winning acclaim from many for her work. The couple seemed happy and content, and for this reason, most of Washington was shocked and surprised at the circumstances surrounding Clover's death.

On Sunday morning, December 6, 1885, Henry went to the dentist with a toothache. When he returned to the house, he discovered that a neighbor who had come calling was standing outside, knocking on the door. Henry knew that she had been expected and so he was surprised that his wife had not come to the door. He immediately unlocked it and went inside, running up the stairs to Clover's bedroom. He burst inside to find his wife lying on the floor in a stupor in front of the fireplace. She never regained consciousness and died a short time later. Clover had swallowed a mixture of potassium cyanide, which would have caused a painful and excruciating death. Why would this vibrant woman have committed suicide?

There have been many theories. It was said that during the last years of her marriage, Clover suffered from an upper respiratory infection that was often exacerbated by Washington's unhealthy climate. This condition, along with the death of her father in the spring of 1885, could have contributed to a lingering depression that caused her to take her own life.

Was this really the case? No one knows for sure and Henry Adams was not talking. He said almost nothing about Clover's death and his bizarre, reclusive behavior only fanned the flames of the gossips. Many began to suggest that perhaps Clover had been murdered. Was this an unjust accusation, generated by the rumor mill? Perhaps, but there were those who pointed out the fact that Henry was also very familiar with darkroom chemicals, like potassium cyanide, and in fact had introduced Clover to photography in the first place. Many years later, after Adams had died, his secretary and niece were looking through his desk, searching for funeral instructions, and found "a partially filled bottle of potassium cyanide, the instrument of Clover's suicide." Was this merely a coincidence?

Shortly after Clover's death, Adams moved out of the house that he had shared with his wife and took up residence in one side of a duplex that he and Clover had been building with John and Clara Hay. Clover was laid to rest in Rock Creek Cemetery and Henry, adding to the rumors of his strangeness, ordered that no stone or marker of any kind should be placed on the grave. He commissioned Augustus Saint Gaudens to create a monument for it and told the sculptor: "No attempt is to be made to make it intelligible to the average mind."

While the statue was being created, Adams ignored remarks from neighbors, hints in newspaper columns and rumors of murder being spread by gossips. He continued his writing, devoting himself completely to historical research. He stayed away from most of his old friends, parties and social and political events, and instead traveled extensively. Six months after Clover's death, Adams and the artist John La Farge departed for Japan. Adams returned in time to be at his father's deathbed in November 1886 and then left again. More travels followed, notably a trip to Polynesia, again with La Farge, in 1890.

Strangely, Adams also made every effort to obliterate his wife from memory. He burned all of her diaries and her letters from her father and her friends. He even burned his own journals and every photograph of Clover that he could find. When his autobiography, *The Education of Henry Adams*, was published in 1918, the gossip started again. Adams wrote

The eerie memorial placed on the grave of Marian Adams. *Library of Congress.*

absolutely nothing of his marriage and the name of Marian Adams was nowhere to be found in the Pulitzer Prize-winning book.

When the statue by Saint Gaudens was finished, Adams was given a masterpiece of melancholy and despair. Adams announced that he would place it in the cemetery, but he was met with resistance from officials. They did not feel that it was a fitting memorial, but Adams persisted and eventually he won. The statue was never given an inscription and not even an official name. It was said that Henry once referred to it as "The Peace of God" but he didn't like people calling it "Grief," which was largely how the statue was dubbed, thanks to its creepy nature. Saint Gaudens had used both men and women for the model and had draped the figure in a long robe, darkly shading the face.

It was said that Henry was obsessed with the monument and would sit in front of it for hours at a time. Years later, a letter to an old friend made one of the very few mentions that Henry ever made to Clover and her death. He wrote:

> *[O]cean of sordidness and restless suburbanity has risen over the very steps of the grave, and for the first time, I suddenly asked myself when I could endure lying there listening to that dreary vulgarity forever, and whether I could forgive myself for condemning my poor wife to it. The grave has become a terror.*

Adams spent the last of his years in Washington surrounded by his nieces and visited by a new generation of America's social and political elite. He died quietly in his home on March 26, 1918, and was buried in Rock Creek Cemetery, next to Clover. No stone marked his resting place, other than the eerie monument that was created as a grim reminder to the memory of his wife.

What thoughts gripped the mind of Henry Adams after his wife's suicide? Was it merely grief, strangely expressed by a man who did not want to show emotion? Or was it something else, something darker, which remains a mystery to this day?

Aurelia Dreyfus & the Dot King Murder

One of Washington's most perplexing unsolved murders took place in 1929 when a woman named Aurelia Dreyfus plunged to her death from a pavilion overlooking the river at the Potomac Boat Club. Her killer remains unknown, but strangely her death was likely not the first to be carried out by this man. For the murder of Ms. Dreyfus will forever be linked to the more famous and more violent murder of a woman named Dot King.

Dot King was born as Dorothy Kennan and she came from an impoverished, New York slum family. She wouldn't stay with her family for long. In 1915, at the age of nineteen, the short but attractive blue-eyed blond left home to become a model in a Fifth Avenue dress shop. She gained a reputation as a showgirl, but there is no record of her ever appearing in any shows, including the famous *Ziegfeld Follies*, where most said she had a prime role.

Dot became a Broadway fixture and was escorted everywhere by millionaires and theater magnates. She became the epitome of the Jazz Age "flapper" with her bobbed hair, dancing, partying and drinking her way through the New York of the early 1920s. She became a speakeasy hostess after Prohibition became law and her name began to appear in gossip columns, where she was often referred to as the "Broadway Butterfly." With this fleeting fame came money, mostly from high-dollar escorts and the inevitable sugar daddies.

One night in a hotel on lower Fifth Avenue, she attracted the attention of a short, stocky, gray haired man of about fifty. He introduced himself as "John Marshall." He had a companion with him, a secretary named John Wilson. Dot and Marshall had an immediate connection—he loved her good looks and fabulous body and she loved his thick wallet.

Marshall set Dot up in an expensive apartment at 144 West 57th Street and bought her jewels, furs, automobiles, lavish food and drink and gave her boatloads of cash, usually $1,000 bills that he tucked under her pillow. His secretary always accompanied Marshall when he called on Dot, but he seldom stayed for long.

When not entertaining Marshall, Dot spent almost every night carousing through Manhattan's lively speakeasies. In one of them, she met and became enamored of a Latin gigolo named Santos Guimares, a man with no

Dot King, the "Broadway Butterfly."
Library of Congress.

income other than what he received from admiring women. Unknown to Dot, Guimares was a fugitive from the law in Boston where he had been indicted by a grand jury for dealing in fake stocks. But Dot was so infatuated with the young man that she allowed him to move into her apartment. He was careful to make himself scarce whenever Marshall came to call. Dot furnished all of Guimares's clothes and gave him large amounts of the money that Marshall gave to her.

Unknown to Dot, Guimares was also seeing a rich socialite named Aurelia Dreyfus, who was also supporting him. She refused to listen to the idea that he was not faithful to her and went out of her way to ignore his transgressions, including the times that he beat her in a drunken rage. When her friends saw the marks and bruises on her arms and body, they urged her to get rid of him. But Dot clung desperately to Guimares, assuring her friends that he was going to marry her someday.

But she soon discovered that love can be brutal, as well as blind.

On the evening of March 14, 1923, Marshall and his secretary, Wilson, came calling at Dot's apartment around 7:30 p.m. The three of them went out for the evening and Dot's maid, Ella (Billie) Bradford, left to go home a short time later. Around midnight, Dot, Marshall and Wilson entered the elevator and the operator, John Thomas, took them to the top floor where the apartment was located. A few moments later, Thomas took only Wilson back down again.

Billie Bradford arrived for work the next morning around 11:30 a.m. As she entered the apartment, she saw two coats on the floor of the small reception room. She picked them up and then walked on toward the bedroom to see if Dot needed anything from her right away. When she walked in, she found Dot lying crumpled on the bed, turned onto her left side. Her head was partially buried under a pillow. Her left arm was twisted behind her back and had been left pushed up between her shoulder blades. Her right hand, with fingers curled into a loose fist, was dangling from the side of the bed. Billie reached for Dot's foot and lightly touched it with her fingers.

The flesh was cold. Dot King was dead.

When Billie looked around, she realized that the apartment had been ransacked. Jewelry and money had been stolen and all of Dot's private letters were missing, save for one torrid piece of correspondence that had been given to her by John Marshall. It read: "Darling Dottie—Only two days before I will be with you. I want to see you, o so much! And to kiss your pretty pink toes."

The maid spotted a pair of men's yellow silk pajamas nearby and she stuffed them under a cushion of the couch in the living room before running to call the police. She later told the investigating officers that the pajamas belonged to Mr. Marshall.

Detectives who arrived at the scene first thought that Dot had committed suicide, but Chief Medical Examiner Dr. Charles D. Norris stated that she had been murdered. Her arm had been brutally twisted behind her back and she had been beaten. Norris also noticed that Dot's nose, eyes and cheeks had been scratched, and that burns around her mouth indicated that she had been chloroformed. The scratches had been caused when a wad of cotton, which was later found under the bed covers, had been roughly placed over her face. Norris estimated that her death had occurred early that morning, between 7:00 and 7:30 a.m.

As the investigation continued, detectives learned that the entrance door had not been forced. Only two keys to the door existed and they belonged to Dot and Billie Bradford. Dot had apparently let her killer inside, and when he left he could have chosen several routes besides the elevator where he would have been spotted by John Thomas.

The mystery took a sensational turn a few days later, when the real identity of Dot's benefactor, John Marshall, was revealed. His real name was J. Kearsley Mitchell and he was the son-in-law of Edward T. Stotesbury, the famous multimillionaire. He confessed that he had been supporting Dot, but under no circumstances had he killed her. He told the police that he had taken her to dinner on March 14 around 7:30 p.m. and had returned to her apartment around midnight. He left at 2:30 a.m. and told the police that he had not used the elevator but had gone down the back stairs instead. This was the reason, he explained, that the elevator operator did not remember seeing him leave.

Even though Mitchell was initially the prime suspect in the murder, the police released him, leading many to speculate that his wealth and power managed to get him out of a tight spot. Even so, Mitchell's involvement in the affair ruined him socially, and he and his family soon sailed for Europe, avoiding any additional notoriety.

The police went looking for friends and acquaintances of Dot King, and it was not long before they found Santos Guimares. Billie Bradford recalled that Dot had called Guimares on March 14 and told him that Mitchell had given her a $1,000 Liberty bond, $500 in cash and a diamond and jade bracelet. The cash and bond were not found in the apartment after the murder and neither was the bracelet.

When the police questioned Guimares, he claimed that he had spent the evening with friends and then had gone to his suite at the Embassy Hotel around 2:30 a.m. He said that he had telephoned Dot just before he went to bed but there had been no answer. He spent the night with a woman, who turned out to be Aurelia Dreyfus, and then had breakfast with her the next morning. Even though the hotel manager could not find a breakfast check signed by Guimares, and no waiter remembered serving him, Aurelia Dreyfus confirmed his alibi. Santos, she said, had been with her all night and during the morning hours. The police had no choice but to release Guimares, and they developed a robbery theory, surmising that two men might have broken into the apartment and made off with her cash and jewels.

The murder of the "Broadway Butterfly" was a nine-day wonder but it eventually faded from the headlines. It remained an open case, though, and a few years later, the press was excited to hear that there could be new developments.

These developments emerged after the death of Aurelia Dreyfus.

On March 29, 1929, Aurelia came to Washington to visit her family. The next evening, she and several family members attended a dance at the Potomac Boat Club. The dance had a tragic ending for Aurelia, for just as the orchestra was playing "Home, Sweet Home" at 1:00 a.m., she was found mortally wounded on the rocky riverbank. It appeared that she had fallen from a pavilion that was located about twenty feet above.

Aurelia's family refused to believe that it had been an accident. On Monday, October 21, her father, Karl Fischer, asserted that she had not fallen—she had been pushed. Apparently, she had recently confessed to her family that she had lied when she had backed Guimares's alibi in the Dot King murder. Guimares had not been with her at the hotel in the morning. Her family insisted that she contact the police, and apparently she swore out an affidavit that admitted that she perjured herself when providing Guimares with the alibi. The paper was found in her belongings after her death. The document, unfortunately, gave no specific details about an actual murder, and investigators, who could not prove that Guimares pushed Aurelia from the balcony, released the gigolo after a routine interrogation.

Thanks to the Washington murder, the authorities began delving into the Dot King investigation once again. In the ensuing grand jury investigation, Aurelia's mother testified that her daughter told her that it had cost $100,000 to hush up the King case. She did not reveal how her daughter knew this information. Thanks to this, along with the other questions that remained, the jury never made any progress with indictments. They simply could not connect Guimares to the murder of Aurelia Dreyfus—or even to Dot King—with any certainty.

During the proceedings and after, Mrs. Anna Keenan, Dot's mother, insisted that Guimares had murdered her daughter and plagued the press for years to pursue the matter.

Guimares drifted for years after Aurelia's death. He had married, divorced and spent three years in prison for swindling. Eventually, he married a wealthy Miami widow but she divorced him after six years. According to her complaint, he had frequently threatened to kill her.

Guimares died in 1953 without ever revealing just what he knew about the two murders. To this day, no one is quite sure who killed the "Broadway Butterfly" or the wealthy socialite who died in Washington. It's likely that the two cases will never be solved.

The Speck of Dust Murder

The Killing of Ruth Reeves

Years before the idea of forensic detection, fingerprints and trace evidence became commonplace, the murder of a Washington woman was solved not only by the efforts of police detectives, but also by scientists who used laboratories and test tubes to track down her killer.

Ruth Reeves's body was discovered on September 8, 1958, when three young boys decided to do some late afternoon fishing along the banks of the Anacostia River near the East Capitol Street Bridge in Washington. Their lines were cast out in the water and soon they were startled by what they assumed must be the largest fish they had ever caught! One of the poles bent nearly in half as the boy frantically tried to reel his catch, but when it broke the water, they made a gruesome discovery. The hook had snagged on the body of a woman and she was pulled from the murky water.

A passing police officer heard the terrified screams of the boys and hurried down the riverbank. He called for backup and soon the officers were pulling the body from the water. She was dressed in pajamas and she had been tied at the hands and feet with thick, metal wire. Someone had also tied a concrete block to her leg in hopes of weighting her down, likely never imagining that a young boy's fishing hook would pull her to the surface. Other than a cheap ring on her finger, there was nothing with which the police could identify her. A fingerprint check revealed nothing, and a search through missing persons reports revealed that nothing had been filed that matched her description. The investigation ground to a halt.

It's possible that the lady in the river would have never been identified if not for John E. Sulhoff, a building engineer for the International Bank for Reconstruction. Sulhoff happened to see a news story regarding the unidentified body and he wondered if it could have been that of Ruth Reeves, an elevator operator at his building. Ruth, a normally punctual and completely dependable woman, had failed to appear the weekend before to operate one of the elevators for the bank building. Sulhoff contacted the police about his suspicions and he was asked to come down to the morgue to take a look at the body. He made a positive identification. It was Ruth Reeves, the missing elevator operator. The police soon learned that she was thirty-eight years old, and in addition to working at the bank building, she also worked in a government building cafeteria in Virginia.

Detectives were sent to Ruth's apartment but they found nothing amiss. They searched the place, but the only item of interest noted was a photograph of Ruth and a man sitting on a desk. A neighbor remembered the man in the photo, which led to him being identified as Philmore Clarke, a carpenter who worked on various government construction projects. Investigators discovered that Clarke was not at work—he had gone on vacation two days before Ruth's body had been found in the river.

As they searched for him, they began to uncover some interesting—and disturbing—information. Clarke had not been dating Ruth for several weeks before her death. She had a new boyfriend and had cut off the relationship with Clarke. He was reportedly angry about that. When detectives visited Clarke's home, they found that several concrete slabs that made up a low wall in front of the house were missing, and eerily, the remaining slabs were identical to the one that had been tied around Ruth's leg. Further, inside of the house was a large spool of wire, which matched the wire that had bound Ruth and attached the concrete to her leg. Detectives began staking out the house and waited for Clarke to return.

On Tuesday night, September 9, Clarke strolled casually up to the house. Detectives said that he was whistling, as if he didn't have a care in the world. He was quickly taken into custody and then to headquarters for interrogation. Clarke had nothing to say. When he was informed that

Ruth had been killed, he sighed and shook his head. He didn't know anything about it, he told detectives.

During the questioning that followed, Clarke denied that he was angry with Ruth and claimed that he had never threatened her after they had broken up, which was the opposite of what some of her friends had told police. He also told the detectives that he had last seen Ruth the previous Sunday, when she had called him and asked him to pick up some groceries for her. According to Clarke, he had dropped them off at noon and that was the last time that he had seen her.

When detectives asked Clarke about the "loud thumping" noises that neighbors reported coming from Ruth's apartment, he denied knowing anything about them. They also asked him about reports of his car being seen outside Ruth's place on the night that she died. Clarke claimed that the car was not his, that it belonged to a friend who had joined the service and left it with a girl that he knew. Clarke admitted that he used the car sometimes, but just before Ruth's murder he had left it parked on the street. When the police asked him where the car was now, he shrugged and said that he guessed that it had been stolen.

After that, the interrogators began revealing the more damning evidence against him. They told him of what they had found at his house, the concrete slab and the spool of wire, and how it had matched the items found with Ruth's body. Clarke laughed at them, and again he shook his head. He told the officers that it was obvious that someone else had killed Ruth and was trying to frame him for her murder.

Detectives were thrown off. They knew that the cement blocks and the spool of wire would look bad for Clarke in court but they lacked the real evidence to place him at the scene of the crime. In addition, the man had an alibi. He claimed that he was in bed with his new girlfriend at the exact time that the police said he dumped Ruth's body in the river. When she was confronted by the investigators, she backed up Clarke's story.

Captain Lawrence Hartnett of Washington's Homicide Squad was not about to give up on the case. The Oldsmobile that Clarke had been driving was found a few days later, parked a few blocks from the man's home. Hartnett ordered it to be impounded and for technicians to painstakingly vacuum the car and take everything in to be examined at the FBI laboratory.

The lab techs found specks of dust in the car, tiny bits of black silica slag. They also found similar dust fragments on Ruth's pajamas and on a pair of shoes that belonged to Clarke. The evidence seemed important—but no one knew why. According to the FBI lab, such residue could only be found in industrial furnaces that maintained incredibly high temperatures.

Hartnett and his detectives returned to the Anacostia riverbank where Ruth's body had been dragged from the water. They took dozens of samples of soil from the riverbank and took it to the lab. The chemists tested them and found that the black silica slag was definitely present. A canvas of power plants proved successful when they found that the Potomac Electric Power Company's furnaces produced the peculiar residue. The waste material was trucked to the very spot where the body had been found and was dumped in the river. The evidence was circumstantial, but it linked Clarke to the scene and he was arrested, indicted and brought to trial. By that time, lab technicians had also found a blood spot on the floor of the Oldsmobile that matched Ruth's blood type.

Thanks to the forensic scientists, as well as homicide detectives, the prosecution was able to prepare a strong case against Clarke. Captain Hartnett believed that Clarke had told the truth about visiting Ruth on the Sunday afternoon that she supposedly asked for groceries—but he had strangled her when she refused to see him again. He carefully cleaned up the apartment and then locked all of the doors and windows when he left. That night, after his new girlfriend fell asleep, he returned to Ruth's apartment, bringing a concrete slab and the spool of wire with him.

After he took the body from the apartment, Clarke drove to the river and tied the concrete slab to Ruth's leg. The weight of the body and the slab were so great that he had to drag the body from the car trunk to the river, coating Ruth's pajamas with the black dust. It was only by chance that Clarke had selected the section of the riverbank where the slag had been dumped, which was something that he did not notice in the dark.

When the prosecutors entered the courtroom on December 9, 1958, they were shocked to learn that Clarke had decided to enter a "guilty" verdict. The defense attorneys had taken the prosecution up on an offer of second-degree murder, which meant less time for the defendant to spend in prison. He received a sentence of up to twenty-five years in prison, but avoided a life term and even a possible death penalty.

Clarke's guilty plea saved the state a costly trial and also saved them from having to admit that, despite the technical evidence, they had no eyewitness testimony to link Clarke to the crime. In 1958, this still counted for more than all of the forensic evidence that could be gathered. Luckily, times would change and it would be learned that dogged police work and painstaking laboratory work could be combined to solve even the most difficult crimes—a fact proven by the case when specks of dust revealed a murderer.

Notes

1. Charles Paul Freund, *Washington Post*, August 13, 1989.
2. *Albany Register*, 1804.
3. Burke Davis, *Old Hickory: A Life of Andrew Jackson* (New York, NY: Dial Press, 1977).
4. Thomas Keneally, *American Scoundrel* (New York, NY: Doubleday, 2002).
5. Ibid.
6. Ibid.
7. Lloyd Lewis, *Myths After Lincoln* (New York, NY: Harcourt, Brace and Co., 1929).

Bibliography

Alexander, John. *Ghosts: Washington Revisited.* Atglen, PA: Schiffer Books, 1998.

Aron, Paul. *Unsolved Mysteries of American History.* Hoboken, NJ: John Wiley & Sons, 1997.

Ayres, Thomas. *That's Not in my American History Book.* Lanham, MD: Taylor Trade Publishing, 2000.

Bishop, Jim. *The Day Lincoln was Shot.* New York, NY: Random House, 1955.

Brookhiser, R. *America's First Dynasty: The Adamses 1735–1918.* New York, NY: Free Press, 2002.

Conroy, Sarah Booth. *Refinements of Love.* New York, NY: Pantheon Books, 1993.

Davis, Burke. *Old Hickory: A Life of Andrew Jackson.* New York, NY: Dial Press, 1977.

Davis, Kenneth C. *Don't Know Much About History.* New York, NY: Harper Collins, 1990.

Donald, David Herbert. *Lincoln.* New York, NY: Simon & Schuster, 1995.

Evans, C. Wyatt. *The Legend of John Wilkes Booth.* Lawrence, KS: University Press of Kansas, 2004.

Farquar, Michael. *Treasury of Great American Scandals.* New York, NY: Penguin, 2003.

Garrison, Webb. *The Lincoln No One Knows.* Nashville, TN: Rutledge Hill Press, 1993.

Guttridge, Leonard F., and Ray A. Neff. *Dark Union.* Hoboken, NJ: John Wiley & Sons, 2003.

Hanchett, William. *The Lincoln Murder Conspiracies*. Urbana, IL: University of Illinois Press, 1983.

Hazelton, George C. *The National Capitol: Its Architecture, Art, and History*. New York, NY: J.F. Taylor & Company, 1903.

Higham, Charles. *Murdering Mr. Lincoln*. Beverly Hills, CA: New Millennium Press, 2004.

James, Marquis. *The Life of Andrew Jackson*. Indianapolis, IN: Bobbs-Merrill, 1938.

Jameson, W.C. *Unsolved Mysteries of the Old West*. Plano, TX: Republic of Texas Press, 1999.

Keneally, Thomas. *American Scoundrel*. New York, NY: Doubleday, 2002.

Kunhardt, Dorothy Meserve, and Phillip Kunhardt Jr. *Twenty Days*. Secaucus, NJ: Castle Books, 1965.

Kunhardt, Phillip B., Jr., Phillip Kunhardt III, and Peter Kunhardt. *Lincoln*. New York, NY: Alfred A. Knopf, Inc., 1992.

Levins, Peter. "The Broadway Butterfly." *American Weekly*. N.d.

Lewis, Loyd. *Myths After Lincoln*. New York, NY: Harcourt, Brace & Co., 1929.

Mogelever, Jacob. *Death to Traitors*. New York, NY: Doubleday, 1960.

Nash, Jay Robert. *Almanac of World Crime*. New York, NY: Bonanza Books, 1986.

———. *Bloodletters and Badmen*. New York, NY: M. Evans & Co. Inc., 1973, 1995.

———. *Murder, America*. New York, NY: Simon & Schuster, 1980.

———. *Open Files*. New York, NY: McGraw-Hill, 1983.

Oates, Stephen B. *With Malice Toward None*. New York, NY: Harper & Row Publishers, Inc., 1977.

Pringle, Henry F. *Theodore Roosevelt*. New York, NY: Konecky & Knonecky, 1931, 2003

Remini, Robert. *Andrew Jackson and the Course of American Democracy*. New York, NY: Harper & Row, 1984.

———. *Andrew Jackson and the Course of American Freedom*. New York, NY: Harper & Row, 1981.

———. *Andrew Jackson and the Course of Empire*. New York, NY: Harper & Row, 1977.

Roscoe, Theodore. *The Web of Conspiracy*. New York, NY: Prentice Hall, 1959.

Schlesinger, Arthur. *The Age of Jackson*. New York, NY: Little Brown, 1945.

Shenkman, Richard, and Kurt Reiger. *One-Night Stands with American History*. New York, NY: Harper Collins, 2003.

Steers, Edward, Jr. *Blood on the Moon: The Assassination of Abraham Lincoln.* Lexington, KY: The University Press of Kentucky, 2001.

Stern, Phillip Van Doren. *The Man Who Killed Lincoln.* N.p., 1939.

Stewart, John. *Early Maps and Surveyors of the City of Washington, D.C.* Lexington, KY: University Press of Kentucky, 1899.

Stimpson, George. *A Book about American Politics.* New York, NY: Harper & Brothers, 1952.

Tally, Steve. *Almost America.* New York, NY: Harper Collins, 2000.

Taylor, Troy. *The Haunted President.* Decatur, IL: Whitechapel Press, 2005.

———. *Spirits of the Civil War.* Decatur, IL: Whitechapel Press, 1999.

Trostel, Scott D. *The Lincoln Funeral Train.* Fletcher, OH: Cam-Tech Publishing, 2002.

Vankin, Jonathan, and John Whalen. *70 Greatest Conspiracies of All Time.* New York, NY: Harper Collins, 1998.

Vowell, Sarah. *Assassination Vacation.* New York, NY: Simon & Schuster, 2005.

Walker, Dale. *Legends & Lies: Great Mysteries of the American West.* New York, NY: Forge Books, 1997.

Weichmann, Louis J. *The True History of the Assassination of Abraham Lincoln & the Conspiracy of 1865.* New York, NY: Alfred A. Knopf, 1975.

Wills, G. *Henry Adams & The Making of America.* New York, NY: Houghton Mifflin, 2005.

Winkler, H. Donald. *Lincoln and Booth.* Nashville, TN: Cumberland House, 2003.